Introduction to Geography:
Where in the World Do Muslims Live?

A Supplementary Social Studies Unit for Grade Four

Written by Susan Douglass

Illustrated by Abdelmuttalib Fahema

Goodwordkidz

Helping you build a family of faith

First published 1995 by
The International Institute of Islamic Thought (IIIT)
500 Grove St., 2nd Floor
Herndon, VA 20170-4735, USA
Tel: (1-703) 471 1133 / Fax: (1-703) 471 3922
E-mail: iiit@iiit.org / URL: http://www.iiit.org

First published by Goodword Books in 2003
Reprinted 2004
in arrangement with The International Institute of Islamic Thought
© The International Institute of Islamic Thought 1995

Goodword Books Pvt. Ltd.
1, Nizamuddin West Market
New Delhi 110 013
e-mail: info@goodwordbooks.com
Printed in India

www.goodwordbooks.com

INTERNATIONAL INSTITUTE OF ISLAMIC THOUGHT (IIIT)

Islamic School Book Project

IIIT is a cultural and intellectual foundation registered in the United States of America in 1981 with the objectives of providing a comprehensive Islamic outlook through elucidating.the principles of Islam and relating them to relevant issues of contemporary thought: regaining the intellectual, cultural, and civilizational identity of the ummah through Islamization of the various disciplines of knowledge, to rectify the methodology of contemporary Islamic thought in order to enable it to resume its contribution to the progress of human civilization and give it meaning and direction in line with the values and objectives of Islam.

IIIT seeks to achieve its objectives by holding specialized academic seminars and conferences, supporting educational and cultural institutions and projects, supporting and guiding graduate and post-graduate studies.

The IIIT Islamic School Book Project supports the writing, publication, and distribution of books and other teaching material for schools as part of its effort to present the true picture of Islam in a factual, objective way. These educational resources, developed under the general guidelines of the IIIT Islamization of Knowledge program, cover the following fields: Islamic Studies, Social Studies, Literature, Science and Mathematics. International collaboration and coordination with teachers, schools and organizations is assured through the International Forum for Education Resources for Islamic English-medium schools.

For more information contact:

The Director
IIIT Islamic School Book Project
International Institute of Islamic Thought (IIIT)
500 Grove St., 2nd Floor,
Herndon, VA 20170-4735, USA
Tel: (1-703) 471 1133 / Fax: (1-703) 471 3922
E-mail: iiit@iiit.org / URL: http://www.iiit.org

ABOUT THE AUTHOR

Susan Douglass is an American-born Muslim who accepted Islam in 1974. She received the Bachelor of Arts in History from the University of Rochester in 1972. She received the Master of Arts in Arab Studies from Georgetown University in 1992. She holds teaching certification in social studies from New York and Virginia.

She has taught in a variety of settings and subjects, beginning with volunteer work in Headstart in 1965. She taught and coordinated art classes in a summer youth program from 1969–72 in Rochester, NY. Since returning to the U.S. in 1984 from extended stays in Germany and Egypt, she resumed work in education. She has taught arts, crafts and story sessions in Muslim summer school programs for several years in Herndon, VA. As teacher and Head of the Social Studies Department at the Islamic Saudi Academy, Alexandria, VA, she taught both elementary and secondary social studies, built a supplementary resource library, and led in preparing a K–12 social studies curriculum utilizing both American and Arab resources for the Academy's accreditation. The current IIIT project was conceived and developed in the classroom. The author is involved in numerous other educational projects, including work as a reviewer and consultant to major textbook publishers in the field of social studies, in addition to various curriculum projects for the Council on Islamic Education in Fountain Valley, CA, including a book, *Strategies and Structures for Presenting World History, with Presentation of Islam and Muslim History as a Case Study* (Amana Publications, 1994).

ADVISORY PANEL MEMBERS

Rahima Abdullah
Elementary Coordinator
Islamic Saudi Academy, Alexandria, VA

Dr. Kadija A. Ali
Educational Projects Coordinator
International Institute of Islamic Thought, Herndon, VA

Jinan N. Alkhateeb
Social Studies Teacher
Islamic Saudi Academy, Alexandria, VA

Mrs. Hamida Amanat
Director of Education
American Islamic Academy
Curriculum Consultant
Al-Ghazaly School, Pine Brook, NJ

Shaker El Sayed
Panel Coordinator
Director of Islamic Schools Departments
Islamic Society of North America, Plainfield, IN

Dr. Tasneema Ghazi
IQRA International Educational Foundation, Chicago, IL

Dr. Zakiyyah Muhammad
Universal Institute of Islamic Education, Sacramento, CA

ACKNOWLEDGEMENTS

Many people's efforts have contributed to producing this series of supplementary units for Social Studies. First, I am grateful to the International Institute of Islamic Thought (IIIT) for placing their confidence in me to undertake a project of this size and for providing all the financial and logistical resources needed for its completion. I would like to thank Dr. Mahmud Rashdan, under whose guidance this project began in 1988. His wisdom helped to set it on a solid foundation. Without constant support and encouragement by Dr. Omar Kasule, project director (1991–present), and Dr. Khadija Ali Sharief, project coordinator (1993–present), this unit would never have met the light of day.

The project has been much enhanced by the members of the Advisory Panel, listed on a separate page. In addition to offering guidance on the project as a whole, they have spent time and detailed effort on each individual manuscript. All are all active education professionals with a broad range of experience and a long list of accomplishments.

May Allah reward my family and grant them patience for sacrificing some degree of comfort so that I, as wife and mother, might realize this goal. I owe special thanks to my husband, Usama Amer, for his constant help with the computer, with Arabic sources and many other matters of consultation. Special appreciation extends to Rahima Abdullah, the fourth grade students and their teachers, Ronna Webb and Mary Nemeth, who field tested this entire unit at the Islamic Saudi Academy. Gratitude is extended to Rabiah Abdullah, whose keen mind and sharp pencil have shaped and pruned text for the whole project, as well as lending her encouragement since its inception.

It has been a pleasure to work on several units with the illustrator, Abdelmuttalib Fahema, who contributed his skill and dedication, bringing enthusiasm and a rare willingness to go the extra mile to research a sketch or detail for accuracy. His training in architecture and his artistic ability, as well as his interest in cultural history particularly enhanced this unit as it has all of the others.

Finally, thanks to the many people at Trimensions Design, Inc. and Kendall/Hunt Publishing Co., who graciously met my many requests and turned complex material into a finished product.

May Allah reward the efforts of sincere workers and of the teachers and students for whom this unit was written.

Susan Douglass
Falls Church, Virginia
October 1995

TABLE OF CONTENTS

Part I

Introductory Notes
for the Teacher

INTRODUCTION

This unit is the fifth in a series of supplementary units for use in Muslim school social studies programs. The underlying assumption is that most such schools will use mainstream curricula as a starting point. While it is certainly desirable and necessary to produce a complete Islamic social studies curriculum, it is a task that is best taken on step by step. In the meantime, it seems most productive to design supplements which are integrated into topics typically studied at a given grade level, while introducing content vital to the development of Muslim identity, values and world view. At the same time, it is hoped that the issues covered in these units are of such importance that they might become integrated into a complete Islamic curriculum.

An important requirement in the design of this supplementary series is that each unit feature skills and concepts typical for the scope and sequence of the social studies curriculum in its grade level. In this way, the teacher can introduce information about the Islamic heritage using material that is well integrated into the existing social studies program. This feature of the design also makes it possible to substitute this material for unsatisfactory or unnecessary material from standard textbooks, to avoid overburdening teacher and students.

PURPOSE AND PLACEMENT OF THE UNIT

This supplementary unit is an introduction to the geography of regions where Muslims live as majorities and a description of the circumstances in which Muslims live as minorities. The focus is more regional than national, so as to overstep the arbitrary modern borders that divide Muslim populations among numerous countries. The unit is designed to complement typical geography surveys offered in elementary social studies curricula. It is designed for grade four, but may be used for grades five and six if the curriculum so requires. Study of this unit may be undertaken after the students have received an introduction to basic geography and map skills. It is probably best undertaken during the second half of the fourth grade year, but since important geography concepts and skills are both introduced and reviewed here, the teacher may be confident to proceed earlier.

The structure of the unit is unique in that the student text is in the form of a play script, whose characters, a teacher and her students, model a cooperative learning experience as they study regions of the world where Muslims live. The main objectives of this unit are to provide students with an overview of the places where Muslims live as majority and minority communities, and to investigate selected aspects of geographic and cultural diversity within the context of Islamic unity.

The unit consists of an eight-lesson student text with teaching suggestions and enrichment activities. Comprehension questions, map skills and worksheets accompany the text for concept reinforcement and skill building. While the unit is designed for flexibility, it is recommended that the students be exposed to the entire student text. If time does not allow extensive study of the unit materials, the teacher may select only basic material from the teaching suggestions rather than covering these with depth and enrichment.

Where in the World Do Muslims Live? is a script for a learning play. The play is set in the classroom of a Muslim elementary school in the United States. Most of the information given is voiced by the students as they present reports and projects and work with maps. Their teacher asks questions, guides discussion, adds information and helps the students with research tasks.

The student text is divided into eight sections ranging from 2¹/₂ to 10 text pages. Each section is a lesson that covers an aspect of the question. In the course of their investigations, students learn how many, where and how Muslims live in various regions of the world. They are also introduced to a number of important terms and concepts of geography study, based upon the Five Themes and Six Essential Elements identified in the National Geography Standards*:

1. Location	1. Seeing the world in spatial terms
2. Place	2. Places and regions
3. Human environment interaction	3. Physical systems
4. Movement	4. Human systems
5. Regions	5. Environment and society
	6. Applying geography

Issues from ecology, economics and cultural studies are raised in this context. Through the text, questions and teaching suggestions, students are guided in the use of various maps, atlases and other reference materials. **A wall- or poster-size physical map of the world and/or laminated markable maps and/or individual classroom atlases should be available to accompany this unit.**

What Is This Book About? sets the scene and introduces the topic of the unit. The cast of characters and their countries of origin are listed.

Section 1 introduces the concept of the unit and the characters in the play. Basic geography definitions and important concepts are reviewed or introduced. Students open the discussion of world population.

Section 2 relates the class discussion and study about the map *The Muslim World* (Islamic Foundation, Leicester, U.K., 1994), showing the percentage of Muslim population in each country. Relevant concepts for discussing population are introduced. The actual map used is provided in the unit binder.

Section 3 relates reports on group research using physical maps of regions where Muslims live, and topic books from the library. The section provides information on landforms and bodies of water, climate, and location of countries.

Section 4 is a discussion of resource use in Muslim regions, including the concepts of rural and urban population, agricultural and industrial products, water use and underground resources. Relevant environmental issues are also mentioned.

---

* *Geography for Life: The National Geography Standards*, Nat'l Center for Geography Education (at UCLA), 1994.

Section 5 continues the investigation of "location" as a geography theme, showing how location can be a resource that provides a living for people. The students investigate common elements in the geographic settings of cities, and use maps to locate and quantify cities in Muslim regions.

Section 6 relates the class investigation of human resources, and their importance for countries' development. Various types of jobs are discussed. The lesson introduces the concept of labor migration into and out of Muslim regions, as well as the economic reasons behind it.

Section 7 relates the discussion of distinctive features of Muslim communities, including aspects of Islam in everyday life, differing masjid architecture, educational institutions and charity. Several regions of conflict or religious discrimination that affect Muslims are touched upon from the perspective of students whose families are from those places.

Section 8 relates the class investigation of cultural similarities and differences among Muslims in various regions. The students stage a culminating festival for the entire school, parents and neighboring community, including a bazaar of Muslim arts and crafts, a show with story- and joke-telling, and a buffet of foods from Muslim lands.

Various support materials are provided with the unit, including a large wall map of *The Muslim World* (Islamic Foundation, Leicester, U.K., 1994) and a poster showing Muslim institutions in the United States, *Muslims in the United States* (American Muslim Council, Washington, D.C., 1995), with an activity to add information to the map. In addition to lesson plans and enrichment activities, projects for varying skill levels are explained in detail: making models of houses from various lands, making Central Asian caps or other head coverings. The unit as a whole can be taken as a model project, from beginning map study to research and presentation of information, discussion, constructing exhibits, and finally staging a Muslim heritage festival in the school. The teacher may enhance the unit by having his or her students reproduce the activities described in the student text, using available research materials from the library or computer learning aids. Thus, the students will experience first-hand what the characters in the script discovered, and they will find out much more information that space constraints did not allow placing in this unit. This exercise in cooperative learning is a model that can be attempted by other groups on this or any other topic.

SECTION 1

The student will

- List some components of geographic study (see themes and elements).
- Identify and locate the continents.
- Recount approximate world population and Muslim population of the world.
- Explain how proportion of population relates to the whole in various ways.

SECTION 2

The student will

- Use a map key to determine topic and content of a map.
- Define **percent** and explain how it relates to population.
- Express various percentage ranges as numbers, as estimates of "how many in ten" and/or as approximate fractional parts of the whole.
- Express selected fractions and percentages on a pie chart.
- Appreciate the distinction between percentage figures and actual numbers of people.
- Define **majority** and **minority**.
- Tell how a census is conducted (optional).

SECTION 3

The student will

- Define the Islamic concept of **ummah** in simple terms, relate it to the English word "community."
- Tell why it is important to learn about the Muslim **ummah**.
- Use a physical map to get information about landforms and vegetation.
- Describe landforms and climate in Muslim regions of Africa (North and East Africa).
- Describe landforms and climate in Muslim regions of Southwest Asia.
- Describe landforms and climate in Muslim regions of Central Asia.
- Describe landforms and climate in Muslim regions of South and Southeast Asia.
- Describe some places in the Americas, Australia and Europe where Muslims live.

SECTION 4

The student will

- Define **resource** and tell the origin of all resources.
- Identify references in classroom or library where information about countries and their natural resources is found.
- Define **urban** and **rural**, and tell the average proportion of each in Muslim regions (approximately 50:50 overall).

- List the resources needed for agriculture (sunshine, land, water, work).
- Define **irrigation** and list several ways to bring water to crops.
- List several important crops and animals raised in various Muslim regions.
- Identify and locate important rivers and define **source** and **mouth**.
- Locate several river **deltas** in Muslim regions.
- Understand that water supplies are very limited in many Muslim regions, and must be carefully used and shared.
- Describe how water use affects the environment.
- List several important natural resources (petroleum, gas, minerals) and appreciate the economic and environmental impact of their sale and use around the world.
- Read a chart showing categories of industries in Muslim countries.
- Categorize types of manufactured goods (consumer, export, processed materials, and basic [capital] goods that help build the country).

SECTION 5
The student will
- Use maps to locate major cities and associate them with landforms (rivers, coastlines, harbors).
- Explain how **location** can be an important asset to a country (bringing trade and jobs).
- Define **port city** and locate some examples in Muslim regions.
- Define **service job** and list examples from Muslim countries or others.

SECTION 6
The student will
- Explain how people are important resources for a community or country.
- List various categories and kinds of jobs.
- Relate education to skill acquisition and jobs.
- Describe the efforts of governments and communities to educate people.
- List reasons why a country might import workers or export them to other countries. (Optional: List examples of target and source countries of labor migration.)
- Understand that **development** means meeting countries' needs and creating jobs.

SECTION 7
The student will
- List some characteristics and features of everyday life that identify a community as Muslim.
- Identify common elements of belief and practice that Muslim individuals and communities carry out in similar ways.
- Appreciate the importance of learning for Muslims and list ways education is carried out in Muslim communities.

- List some languages spoken by Muslims around the world.
- Identify several regions in which Muslims have suffered lack of tolerance or actual conflict and discuss some of the specific reasons for their suffering.
- Identify ways that Muslims can help preserve Islam and the Muslim community locally and internationally.

SECTION 8

The student will

- Identify differences in way of life (housing, family structure, dress, foods) among Muslim regions.
- List examples of traditional arts and crafts in the Muslim world.
- Use library resources and/or personal interviews to find examples of literary arts from Muslim regions.
- Appreciate the process and results of cooperative learning in a group setting.

The teaching suggestions and activities are an integral part of the unit before you. The text and illustrations alone cannot convey to young students all the information necessary to a well-integrated and comprehensive learning experience. Students of this age level need guidance in organizing and retaining information from their reading. Above all, the students need help relating new learnings to things they already know, enabling them to build up a store of factual information and conceptual understanding, and acquiring the skills to apply it. In the Muslim classroom, the teacher helps the students to see things from a Muslim perspective. The teacher may also need to fill in or help the students to access background information that is too bulky or complex to provide in the student text.

The activities in this unit have been designed to meet these needs, fill in these gaps, or refer to other sources. It is the author's hope that the teaching suggestions are not overlooked as "optional" or burdensome to navigate. Planning time spent reviewing the discussion guide and selecting appropriate activities for comprehension and enrichment is well invested to make the learning experience rewarding in any setting.

The student text is to be reproduced for individual students and taken home as a reminder of their study. **The illustrations and maps may be used as coloring pages.** Teachers may help students bind and decorate individual student booklets with self-made covers, Islamic calligraphy and/or designs. This activity may embrace one or all of the unit segments.

The activities described here are recommended for use with individual sections of the student text *Where in the World Do Muslims Live?* **A wall- or poster-size physical map of the world and/or laminated markable maps and/or individual classroom atlases should be available to accompany this unit.** Specific references are given in the text and bibliography, although any quality map is fine. Mercator map projections, with their significant distortion of the upper northern hemisphere, are to be avoided if possible in favor of an "Equal Area" (Robinson or Eckert), Goode's split-ocean, or other projection adjusted to reflect the continents' relative size. (The quickest way to tell a Mercator projection is the massive enlargement of Greenland.)

The teaching suggestions provide comprehension exercises, development and reinforcement of skills and concepts introduced in the text, and enrichment activities for social studies with springboards to other disciplines. They are designed to offer maximum flexibility in expanding or compressing the unit to fit variable time frames. The suggestions are organized according to sections of the student text, and are labeled by type of activity.

- *PRE-READING:* These activities are done before classroom or individual reading in the student text. They provide background information, define unfamiliar words and establish a receptive frame of mind in the students.

- *COMPREHENSION:* These activities are completed after each section is read. They include questions for classroom discussion and individual work, explanatory background material to be provided by the teacher, and exercises related to understanding content.

- **LEARNING NEW CONCEPTS:** The focus is on comprehension and manipulation of concepts from the social studies disciplines. The concepts are explained, put to use and reinforced in these activities.

- **ACQUIRING SKILLS:** These activities feature social studies skills such as interpreting maps, diagrams and pictures; reading, writing, speaking, thinking and study skills, as well as citizenship.

- **ENRICHMENT:** Activities are offered that build upon the basic lessons, adding depth and enjoyment to the learning experience. They may include art, science, math or computer projects, literature for additional reading, dramatic or role play, Islamic studies or Arabic.

This supplementary unit is designed for flexibility. It may be implemented in its most basic form in a **two- to three-week time period, or it may be extended to four to six weeks,** depending upon the depth of study and the number of enrichment projects undertaken. The teacher may choose to cover some segments lightly, omitting skills and enrichment activities, while covering other segments more exhaustively. Like the other supplementary units in this series, *Where in the World Do Muslims Live?* may be utilized for broader purposes over a longer time period. A wide variety of social studies concepts for the fourth grade year are touched upon and covered in the concept and skills activities.

A skillful teacher will integrate these lessons into the annual curriculum as a whole. In this way, opportunities for comparison and contrast with standard textbook chapters will not be missed. Having the whole year's curriculum in view will also avoid wasting precious learning time by identifying opportunities to substitute this study of Muslim regions for unnecessary or marginally useful materials. Planning across the curriculum will enable the teacher to coordinate math, science, computer studies, literature and Islamic studies with interdisciplinary learning activities from *Where in the World Do Muslims Live?*

BOOKS

Central Asia and the Caucasus after the Soviet Union, Mohiaddin Mesbahi, ed. Gainesville, FL: University Press of Florida, 1994.

Central Asia and Transcaucasia: Ethnicity and Conflict, Vitaly V. Naumkin, ed. Westport, CT: Greenwood Press, 1994.

Geography Across the Curriculum, Dennis and Judy Reinhartz. Washington, DC: National Education Association, 1990.

Geography for Life: The National Geography Standards. Los Angeles, CA: National Center for Geography Education, 1994.

Grollier Multimedia Encyclopedia. Grollier Electronic Publishing, Inc., 1994.

Islam in Asia, Vol. II: Southeast and East Asia, Raphael Israeli and Anthony H. Johns. Boulder, CO: Westview Press, 1984.

Islamic Economic Cooperation, Masudul Alam Choudhury. New York: St. Martin's Press, 1987.

Muslim Minorities in the World Today, M. Ali Kettani. London: Mansell Publishing, Ltd., 1986.

Muslim World Geography and Development, Mushtaqur Rahman, ed. Lanham, MD: University Press of America, Inc., 1987.

People At Work in the Middle East, Christine Osborne. London: B.T. Batsford, Ltd., 1987.

Private Voluntary Organizations in Egypt: Islamic Development, Private Initiative and State Control, Denis J. Sullivan. Gainesville, FL: University Press of Florida, 1994.

The Changing Geography of Africa and the Middle East, Graham P. Chapman and Kathleen Baker, eds. London: Routledge, 1992.

The Changing Geography of Asia, Graham P. Chapman and Kathleen Baker, eds. London: Routledge, 1992.

The Least Developed and the Oil-Rich Countries, Kinbert Raffer and M. A. Mohammed Salih, eds. New York: St. Martin's Press, 1992.

The World of Islam, T. B. Irving. Brattleboro, VT: Amana Books, 1984.

Two Worlds of Islam: Interaction between Southeast Asia and the Middle East, Fred R. von der Mehden. Gainesville, FL: University Press of Florida, 1993.

ARTICLES

"Europe Faces an Immigrant Tide," Peter Ross Range, *National Geographic Magazine,* 183:5 (May 1993), pp. 38–71.

"The Middle East's Water: Critical Resource," Priit Vesilind, *National Geographic Magazine,* 183:5 (May 1993), pp. 38–71.

"The Politics of Population," Elizabeth Sobo, *The Minaret,* 16:4 (Sept./Oct. 1994), pp. 24–28.

Muslim Kaleidoscope: The Magazine for Muslim Children, Amica International, 1201 First Ave. South, Suite 203, Seattle, WA 98134.

Aramco World Magazine

"Muslims in China," Lawton, et al., *Aramco World Magazine*, 36:4 (June/Aug. 1985).

"A City Within a City," passim, *Aramco World Magazine*, 38:5 (Sept./Oct. 1987).

"Muslims in the Caribbean," "Stitches Through Time," "The Nature of the Nile," "The Changing Present," 38:6 (Nov./Dec. 1987).

"Images of Oman," William Tracy, *Aramco World Magazine*, 40:1 (Jan./Feb. 1989).

"Craftsmen of Bahrain," Wendy Levine, *Aramco World Magazine*, 40:2 (Mar./Apr. 1989).

"Egypt's Underwater World," "Lakes of the Rub'Al-Khali," "Crossing the Rub," *Aramco World Magazine*, 40:3 (May/June 1989).

"An Oryx Update," Tillman Durdin & John Lawton, *Aramco World Magazine*, 40:5 (Sept./Oct. 1989).

"Imbaba," Akram Khater, *Aramco World Magazine*, 40:6 (Nov./Dec. 1989).

"Saudi Arabia Yesterday and Today," *Aramco World Magazine*, 40:7 (Exhibition Issue).

"Muslims in the USSR," Lawton, et al., *Aramco World Magazine*, 41:1 (Jan./Feb. 1990).

"Ramadan in Holland," Hillary Keatinge, *Aramco World Magazine*, 41:2 (Mar./Apr. 1990).

"Remaking Istanbul," "Fishing in Pondo," *Aramco World Magazine*, 41:4 (July/Aug. 1990).

"The Pesantren at Surialaya," "Djenne: Living Tradition," *Aramco World Magazine*, 41:6 (Nov./Dec. 1990).

"Images of Afghanistan," "In Harm's Way," *Aramco World Magazine*, 42:3 (May/June 1991).

"On Culture's Loom," "Diving in the Southern Red Sea," "Sudan: Land of the Pyramids," *Aramco World Magazine*, 42:4 (July/Aug. 1991).

"Islam's Path East," passim, *Aramco World Magazine*, 42:6 (Nov./Dec. 1991).

"A Mosque in Islambad," Len McGrane, *Aramco World Magazine*, 43:1 (Jan./Feb. 1992).

"Jabal Ali: Dubai's Gateway to the World," Larry Luxner, *Aramco World Magazine*, 43:2 (Mar./Apr. 1992).

"The Academy of the Rain Forest," "Oman's Unfailing Springs," [traditional irrigation system like qanat], *Aramco World Magazine*, 43:6 (Nov./Dec. 1992).

"The People Persist" [Cham Muslims of Cambodia], "Across the High Atlas" [Morocco], *Aramco World Magazine*, 44:2 (Mar./Apr. 1993).

"An Inventory in Arabia Felix," "Saudi Aramco at Sixty," "Deep Threats" [India], *Aramco World Magazine*, 44:5 (Sept./Oct. 1993).

"Lebanon: Up from the Ashes," "Transports of Delight," *Aramco World Magazine*, 45:1 (Jan./Feb. 1994).

"Islam in Bulgaria," Stephen Lewis, *Aramco World Magazine*, 45:3 (May/June 1994).

"The White Mosques of Jerba," Michael Balter, *Aramco World Magazine*, 45:4 (July/Aug. 1994).

BOOKS FOR STUDENT READING

Arab Folktales, Inea Bushnaq. New York: Pantheon Books, 1986.

Eternal Saudi Arabia, Rick Golt. London: Elk Publications, 1980.

Geography for Every Kid, Janice VanCleave. New York: John Willey and Sons, Inc., 1993.

Goha, Denys Johnson-Davies. Cairo: Hoopoe Books, 1993.

How Much Is a Million? David M. Schwarz (S. Kellog, illus.). New York: Scholastic, Inc., 1985.

Issues . . . Issues . . . Issues: The Palestinians, David McDowall. New York: Gloucester Press, 1986.

Land of Yesterday, Land of Tomorrow: Discovering Chinese Central Asia, Paul, David and Peter Conklin/Brent Ashabranner. New York: Cobblehill Books, 1992.

Pakistan: My Country Series, Bernice and Cliff Moon. New York: Marshall Cavendish, 1986.

Sahara: Vanishing Cultures, Jan Reynolds. San Diego: Harcourt Brace Jovanovich, 1991.

The Childrens' Story Series (Grades 4–6), Uthman Hutchinson. Beltsville, MD.: Amana Publications, 1995.

The Former Soviet States: The Central Asian States, Paul Thomas. Brookfield, CT.: Millbrook Press (Aladdin Books, 1992).

The Land and People of Malaysia & Brunei, John S. Major. New York: Harper Collins Publishers, 1991.

The Magic Stone, G. Naumenko (G. Glagoleva, transl.). Moscow: Mylysh Publ., 1981 (Imported Publications, 320 West Ohio St., Chicago, IL 60610).

Then & Now: Azerbaijan, Mary Rodgers, ed. Minneapolis: Lerner Publications, 1993.

Then & Now: Kazakhstan, Mary Rodgers, ed. Minneapolis: Lerner Publications, 1993.

Then & Now: Tajikistan, Mary Rodgers, ed. Minneapolis: Lerner Publications, 1993.

Then & Now: Turkmenistan, Mary Rodgers, ed. Minneapolis: Lerner Publications, 1993.

Then & Now: Uzbekistan, Mary Rodgers, ed. Minneapolis: Lerner Publications, 1993.

We Live in Kenya, Zulf M. Khalfan and Mohamed Amin. New York: Bookwright Press, 1984.

We Live in Malaysia and Singapore, Jessie Wee. New York: Bookwright Press, 1985.

ATLASES AND MAPS

Muslims in the United States. American Muslim Council, 1212 New York Ave., NW, Suite 400, Washington, D.C. 20005, 1995.

National Geographic Atlas of the World. Washington, DC: National Geographic Society, 1994.

Rand McNally Picture Atlas of the World, Brian Delf. Chicago: Rand McNally, 1991.

Rand McNally Student's World Atlas. Chicago: Rand McNally, 1994.

The Geography Coloring Book, Wynn Kapit. New York: Harper Collins Publishers, 1991.

The M.W.H. Map of the Muslim World, The Muslim Welfare House. London: M.W.H. and Beirut: GEOprojects, 1980.

The Muslim World Map. Leicester, U.K.: The Islamic Foundation, 1994.

Where in the World Do Muslims Live?

Written by Susan Douglass

Illustrated by Abdelmuttalib Fahema

يَٰٓأَيُّهَا ٱلنَّاسُ إِنَّا خَلَقْنَٰكُم مِّن ذَكَرٍ وَأُنثَىٰ وَجَعَلْنَٰكُمْ شُعُوبًا وَقَبَآئِلَ لِتَعَارَفُوٓا۟ إِنَّ أَكْرَمَكُمْ عِندَ ٱللَّهِ أَتْقَىٰكُمْ إِنَّ ٱللَّهَ عَلِيمٌ خَبِيرٌ

O mankind! Lo! We have created you male and female, and have made you nations and tribes that you may know one another. Lo! The noblest of you in the sight of Allah is the best in conduct. Lo! Allah is Knower, Aware.

(Qur'an 49:13)

WHAT IS THIS BOOK ABOUT?

In this book you will find out where and how Muslims live all around the world. This book is written in the form of a play. It tells the story of a project in a Muslim school elementary class. The school is located in the United States. The class is learning about geography when someone asks the question: "Where in the world do Muslims live?" The students, with the help of their teacher, Abla (meaning "older sister") Amina, look for the answer. They discover many things about Muslims, about the world today, and about geography. Most important, the class learns how to cooperate to tackle a big job.

Meet the class now. Join them as they do research, make projects, and interview people to answer their questions. The students in our class are from many different countries. Each of them worked hard on our project. At the end, we had a surprise. Read along with the students and find out!

Scene: Muslim school in the United States, elementary classroom.

Cast of Characters:

1. Student narrator
2. The teacher, Abla Amina
3. Ali (Kenya)
4. Amele (Bosnia)
5. Anas (Egypt)
6. Burhan (Uzbekistan)
7. Fatima (Algeria)
8. Ibrahim (Indonesia)
9. Khadijah (Libya)
10. Muhammad (Oman)
11. Nabil (Pakistan)
12. Nada (Turkey)
13. Nur (China)
14. Omar (Palestine)
15. Rahma (Senegal)
16. Sayyid (Kashmir)
17. Zaid (United States)

Part II
Student Text

MEET THE CLASS

STUDENT NARRATOR: Welcome to our classroom. This year, we have begun to study **geography**. In geography we study different places on the Earth. We study the continents.° We learn about features of the land and water. We learn about the **climate**, or weather throughout the year. We study the people living on Earth. We learn how people use the land and its **resources**. We study how a place and its people change over time.

The class has studied many different countries. Our textbook describes North America and the United States. It also has chapters on South America, Africa, Asia and the other continents. One day, Zaid asked a question.

Zaid: In our book, there are many pictures of people from different countries. In a few pictures, there were Muslims. Sometimes, we could tell by their clothes. Most of the chapters, like South America, North America and Europe, didn't show any pictures of Muslims. Does that mean they don't live there?

Abla Amina: Who knows whether Muslims live in those places?

Muhammad: We know there are Muslims in North America because *we* live here!

° See Worksheets #1a–c.

Fatima: My uncle lives in France. That's in Europe.

Amele: My country is Bosnia. That is in Europe, too. We just came here last year.

Abla Amina: Who else has relatives or friends in other countries?

Nada: My uncle and cousins live in Germany. I have another uncle in Australia.

Rahma: My parents are from Senegal, in Africa. Most of our family lives there now.

Omar: My family is Palestinian. Some of my uncles used to live in Kuwait, but now they are in Jordan.

Nabil: My father and mother came here from Afghanistan.

Nur: My mother's family is in China. We have pictures of them.

Abla Amina: Now we know that there are Muslims in North America, Europe, Africa and Asia. Is that all?

Zaid *[frowning]*:   I know that there are lots of kids in this school from different places. But why don't we read much about Muslims in our books? Are there a lot of Muslims in the world, or not very many? Where in the world do Muslims live?

STUDENT NARRATOR: Abla Amina started asking more questions. She does that all the time. But this time, we didn't know that it would take more than a month to find the answers!

Abla Amina: How can we find out where Muslims live? How can we find out how many there are?

Muhammad: My father told me that there are about 1 billion Muslims!

Abla Amina: That is what I have heard. The world **population (number of people)** is about 5 billion, so how many Muslims is that?

Fatima: That means one out of every five persons in the world is Muslim. Is that many or few?

Nur: China has about one billion people, my mom said, but they're not all Muslims.

Abla Amina: Let me show you how many that is. I have something in the science center that will help us understand. *[She takes out a bag of white beans and a bag of red beans. She measures four jars of white beans and one jar of red beans. She lines them up on the desk.]* Which jar represents the Muslim population of the world?

Zaid: The red jar.

Abla Amina: Correct. This helps us understand how many, but it does not tell us very much. It doesn't tell us whether the Muslims live all together in one part of the world, or whether they live scattered and mixed among the other people.

Zaid: What do you mean?

Abla Amina [pours the white, then red beans into a bowl]: Here, the red beans are not mixed in with the others. They are all close to each other. That is like having a neighborhood where many Muslim families live together. Now, someone mix the beans. *[Zaid stirs them with his hand]* Here, Muslims live scattered in many places. How would that affect the lives of each? Now, class, how can we find out whether Muslims live close together or far apart in the world today?

Khadija: We have a map at home that shows all of the Muslim countries in green.

Abla Amina: Can you bring it in tomorrow, in sha' Allah?

Khadija: I will ask my parents to let us borrow it, in sha' Allah (SWT).

Thinking About Section 1:

1. Why do people who share a common way of life often live close together?

2. What is the total world population? Write it in numbers. Write the Muslim population of the world in numbers. How many zeros does the number have?

MAPS, COLORS AND BIG NUMBERS*

STUDENT NARRATOR: Next day, Khadija brought in the map. It was large, and showed the whole world. Some of the countries were colored dark green. Others were light green. Some were yellow. Other countries were red or tan. The rest of the map was blue, for the water.

Abla Amina: Let's look carefully at the map. How can we find out what the colors mean?

Omar [going to the map]:   The map has a **key**. This one says *"Percent of Muslims in each country's population."* Dark green means over 50%.

Abla Amina: Does everyone know what **"percent"** means? It means **"how many out of every hundred"** people are Muslims. Look at the countries colored dark green. What percent of the people there are Muslims?

Fatima: More than half of the people are Muslims!

Abla Amina: Where are many of those countries located?

Khadija: They're in the middle of the map, almost. Some are in Africa, and some are in *[points to Arabian Peninsula]* . . . is that Asia or what?

Abla Amina [laughing]:   You mean the Arabian Peninsula, where the city of Makkah is located? That is part of Asia. Geographers call it Southwest Asia, because it is a special region.

Omar, trace the green countries from West to East. What shape do they make?

---

* While you read this section, use the map *The Muslim World*, from the Islamic Foundation, Leicester, England, which is included in the binder with this unit.

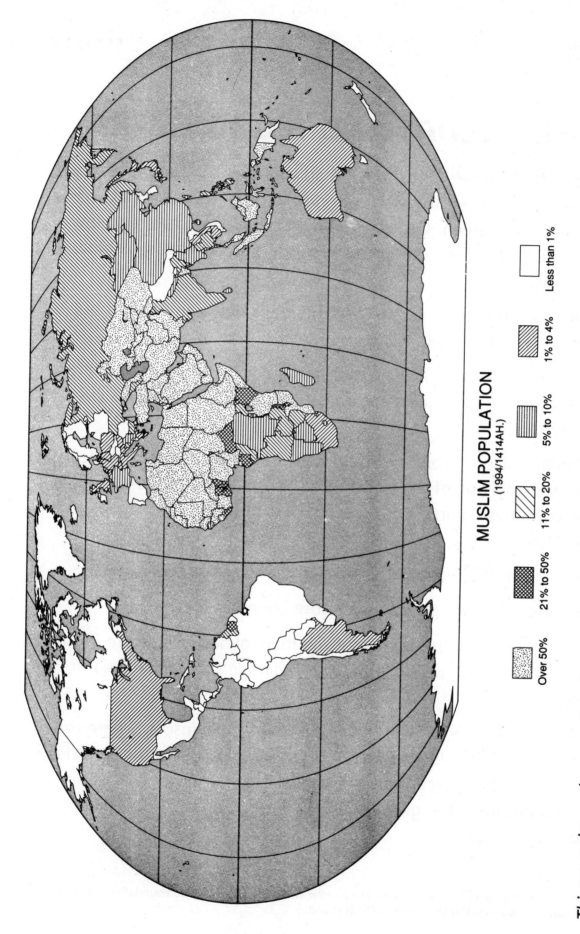

MUSLIM POPULATION
(1994/1414AH.)

Over 50%

21% to 50%

11% to 20%

5% to 10%

1% to 4%

Less than 1%

This map shows the countries of the world. Each country is shaded to show the percentage of Muslims in its population. The map helps us to understand where in the world Muslims live.

Omar: They are a big mass of countries across Africa and into Asia. There are some in the ocean, too.

Muhammad: That's Indonesia! It has a lot of islands. My father went there once. He showed me on the map.

Abla Amina: That's right, Muhammad. What does the medium green color on the map mean?

Anas [going up to the map]:   On the key it says *"21% to 50%."* That means between one quarter and one half of the people in the country are Muslim. One quarter is 25%, but 21% is close to it.

Abla Amina: Good, Anas. Where are those countries?

Zaid: Medium green countries are next to the dark green countries. I see some in Africa, one in Europe and one in South America.

Abla Amina: What is the next lightest color?

Fatima: It is light green. The key says *"11% to 20%."* That is a smaller amount.

Abla Amina: That means 1 out of every 10 people to 2 out of 10. Who can tell us where they are?

Khadija: There are light green countries in Africa and in Asia. After that comes yellow-colored countries. They have only 5% to 10% Muslims.

Abla Amina: Then comes red. Look at the United States. What color is it?

Zaid: It is colored red. That means *"1% to 4%"* Muslim. That isn't very much, is it?

Abla Amina: It can still mean that millions of Muslims live in the country.

Zaid: How could that be?

Abla Amina: Let's look at an example. Algeria, a large country, is dark green. It has about 26 million people, almost all Muslims. Who can find Algeria on the map?

Fatima [pointing]:   Here it is, in Africa.

Abla Amina: China is another very large country. Who can find it, and what color is it?

Nur [pointing]:   It is this big country in Asia. It is colored yellow.

Abla Amina: That color means 5% to 10% percent of the people in China are Muslims. There are more than twice as many Muslims in China—about 60 million—as in Algeria! So less than 10% of the people in China equals more people than 90% of the people in Algeria!

Zaid: Really?! This idea of percent (%) is not so easy!

Abla Amina: I will explain. China, with almost 1 billion people, has a larger population than Algeria. Let's look at it this way. We have a very big pie and a very small one. *[draws two pies on the board]*° Which is more pie, a big piece of the small one, or a small piece of the big one?

Zaid: I want a piece of that big one.

Abla Amina: Me, too. Let's look at another example of countries on our map. Libya is next to Algeria. What color is it?

Fatima: It's dark green. How many people live in Libya?

Abla Amina: I've read that the whole population is about 5 million. We don't know for sure, but there might be more than 6 million Muslims here in the United States! But the U.S. has over 250 million people. It is red colored on the map. Only about 2% of the population here is as many as almost 100% in Libya!

° See Worksheet #2.

The bell rings to end the class: BBBBRRRRRINGGG!

Abla Amina: *Jazakum Allahu khairan!* Thank you for bringing in the map, Khadija. Let's keep it on the wall for a while. I think we still have a lot more work to do.

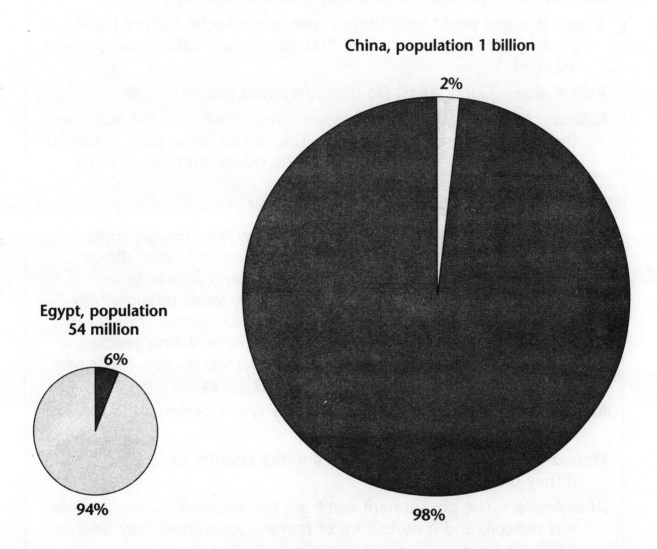

These two circles, or pie charts, show us how much of the population of China and Egypt is Muslim. The percent of Muslims in Egypt (94%) is much larger than in China (2%–4%). However, the pie that represents China's population (1 billion) is much larger than the pie for Egypt (54 million). Which is larger, a small piece of a big pie, or a large piece of a smaller pie?

STUDENT NARRATOR: After class, some students stayed to talk to the teacher.

TAKING A "CENSUS" MEANS COUNTING PEOPLE

Zaid: Why did you say that there "might be" 6 million Muslims in the US? Aren't they sure how many are here? How do countries count people?

Abla Amina: How can we find that out? Who can help?

Anas: We read about counting people in our Social Studies book. *[looks it up]* Here it is! It says, *"The government takes a **census** every 10 years."*

Abla Amina: Good, Anas. Do they just count people?

Fatima: No, they ask lots of questions. You showed us the questions they mailed to everyone's house. They asked about jobs, people's ages, how many bathrooms are in the house, and lots of other things.

Zaid: Do all countries take a—**census**?

Abla Amina: Yes, governments need to know how many people there are, to build enough schools, hospitals and other things. They mail questions to each home. They send people to ask questions, or ask at work and schools. They want to know how many people live in cities, and how many on farms. They try to find out whether there are more old people or young people. *Some governments ask about religion, but others do not. That's why we don't always know how many Muslims are in the population.*

Muhammad: Can they really count every single person and answer everything?

Fatima: What if someone went to another country on a trip? What if they didn't tell the truth?

Abla Amina: The government can't get the information exactly right. It is difficult, and it costs a lot of money. Sometimes they have to be like detectives. They try to make a good guess.

Zaid: What does all that have to do with how many Muslims there are?

Khadija: It means that it's impossible to know exactly how many. *Allahu 'aalam.* God knows!

Thinking About Section 2:

1. What does the map key show?

2. What does *percent* mean?

3. In what library resources can you find out about the population of each country in the world? Pick three countries. Write the name of each and its population.

4. How can you use the *Map of the Muslim World* to estimate, or guess, how many Muslims are in each country, if you know the total population?

5. CALCULATOR ACTIVITY: What is the highest and the lowest possible number of Muslims in Nigeria? Try some other countries.

PLACES WHERE MANY MUSLIMS LIVE

STUDENT NARRATOR: After we talked about the map, more students caught Zaid's question fever. Fatima wanted to know what Chinese Muslims eat. Nabil asked if there were any Eskimo Muslims. Muhammad asked, "Why do we always see camels and sand and palm trees in books about Muslims?" As usual, Abla Amina asked more questions. Now, we really started working!

Abla Amina: You are asking **geography** questions now. You are asking about the places where Muslims live. Let us start a class project. We can try to gather information about Muslims in the world.

Fatima, Muhammad, Omar: That sounds like a lot of work.

Abla Amina: It will be, but it can be fun. It is an important job. Muslims should learn about their community.

Anas: We have a Muslim community here. We have a masjid and a school.

Abla Amina: Yes, but who knows what the biggest Muslim community is called?

Muhammad: It is all the Muslims in the world. In Arabic it means *ummah.*°

Abla Amina: Who knows a *hadith* about the *ummah*?

Rahma: I do. The Prophet said that *the believers have mercy to each other and show each other love and kindness. They are like one body, so that if any part of the body is not well, the whole body shares the fever with it and cannot sleep.* ✩

° See Worksheet #3.
✩ Meaning of the hadith from *Sahih al-Bukhari* 8:40

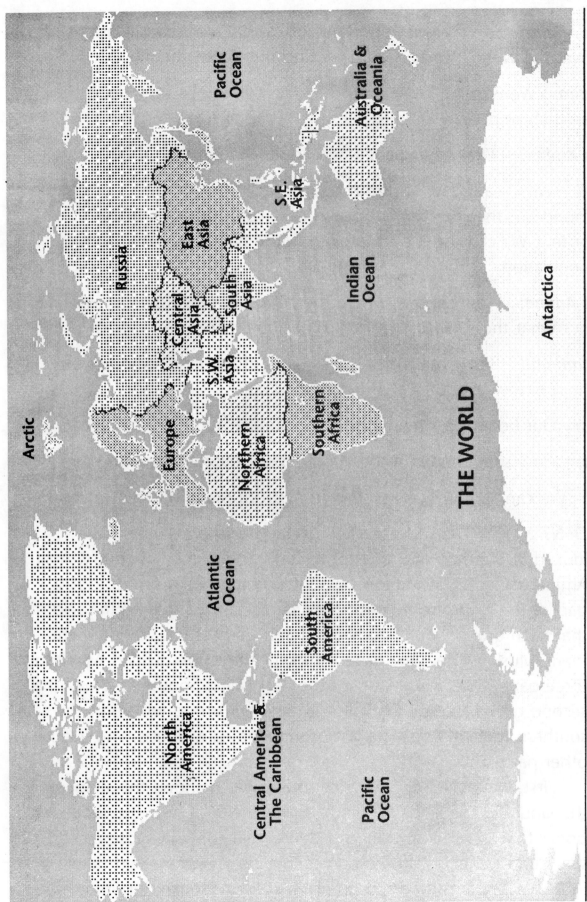

THE WORLD

This world map shows the continents divided into parts, or regions. By studying each region one by one, it is easier to study Allah's very big world.

Abla Amina: So why is it important for us to learn about Muslims all over the world? What should we find out about them?

Khadija: We want to know how they live, what jobs they do, if they are rich or poor.

Abla Amina: What have we learned about the *ummah* so far?

Nabil: We already saw on the map where Muslim countries are. We found out that the percent doesn't tell us if there are many or few. We can use a calculator to figure out how many from the population.

Abla Amina: We looked at where the countries are. How can we find out what those places are like? What other kinds of maps help us?

Muhammad: Some maps show the shape of the land, whether it is high or low, and they show rivers and cities.

Anas: Our book has a map about the climate, too.

Zaid: I saw some books in the library about different countries.

Nur: We can ask our families. We come from many different places.

STUDENT NARRATOR: So the class decided to share the job. We looked at the map and each of us found our family's country. Abla Amina helped to divide the class into groups. Each group took a part of the world from which their family came. Abla Amina said that each group would study a different part of the world where many Muslims live. One group studied Africa. We divided Asia into three parts. One group studied the part called Southwest Asia. The second group studied Central Asia. Another group looked at the southern parts of Asia. The last group studied Muslims who live in other parts of the world.

First, we looked at a **physical map**, which shows the shape of the land and the kinds of things that grow on it. We also looked at books that showed animals and things that grow in those places. We found out about the resources they have. We studied different jobs that Muslims do. Each group of students looked up information in the library. Then the class listened to each group's report. Here is what the class learned:

Africa

Rahma (Senegal): We studied Africa. Most of the Muslim countries are in the wide part of Africa. That is northern Africa. Almost all of the countries in northern Africa are Muslim countries. The narrow part of Africa is southern Africa. In southern Africa, there are fewer Muslim countries. There, Muslims live together with many other groups of people.

Anas (Egypt): Most of northern Africa is covered by the Sahara Desert. It is the largest desert in the world. Even though the countries in the Sahara Desert are very large, few people can live there. Between the desert and the Mediterranean coast of Africa are farm lands. South of the Sahara are grasslands. South of the grasslands are forests. Most of the Muslim countries are in the drier parts. In eastern Africa, there are more grasslands and forests, but parts of it, like Somalia, are also very dry.

Ali (Kenya): We found some books that showed people crossing the Sahara with camels. People raise camels in Somalia and Ethiopia, too. Cars and trucks also transport people and things. Each year, a famous car race crosses the Sahara Desert.

Fatima (Algeria): In northern Africa, there are some important rivers. The Nile River is the longest one in the world. It starts in Uganda and Ethiopia, and goes through Sudan and Egypt. Another important river is the Niger River. It is shaped like a rainbow. It starts in Guinea, then it goes north through Mali. In the middle of Mali, it turns to go south through Niger and Nigeria. In East Africa, there are many small rivers. The Zambezi is another large river. It goes east, through Mozambique.

Ali: There are some high mountains in Africa. The highest one is Mt. Kilimanjaro, between Kenya and Tanzania. I visited it one

Map of Northern Africa

NORTHERN AFRICA

Atlantic Ocean

Europe

Southwest Asia

Indian Ocean

Southern Africa

Morocco

Western Sahara

Tunisia

Algeria

Libya

Egypt

Mauritania

Mali

Niger

Chad

Sudan

Eritrea

Djibouti

Somalia

Ethiopia

Central African Republic

Cameroon

Nigeria

Benin

Togo

Ghana

Burkina

Ivory Coast

Liberia

Sierra Leone

Guinea

Guinea Bissau

Senegal

Gam.

C. V.

Map of Southern Africa

summer with my parents. We saw lots of wild animals in Kenya. Part of Lake Victoria is in Kenya, too. It is one of the biggest lakes in the world. There are also lots of mountains in Ethiopia. There are mountains all over the Sahara Desert. Mountains divide the desert from the coast in North Africa, especially in Morocco and Algeria. Central Africa is a **plateau**. That is high, flat land.

Abla Amina: Thank you for telling us about the geography of Muslim parts of Africa. The next group to report has studied Arabia and Southwest Asia. Since Asia is so large, geographers divide it into parts. There are three parts where many Muslims live. They are Southwest Asia, South Asia and Central Asia [shows them these parts on the map].

Southwest Asia

Omar (Palestine): The biggest part of Southwest Asia is the Arabian Peninsula. It looks like a big boot that is kicking Asia. It is called a **peninsula** because it is surrounded by water on three sides. The Arabian Peninsula is even surrounded on four sides, but it is attached to the land at the top of the boot, front and back.

Muhammad (Oman): At the top of the boot, to the north, are Turkey, Iran, and Iraq. North of these countries are two large seas, the Black Sea and the Caspian Sea. Between the Arabian Peninsula and Iran is a body of water. On maps, it is called the Persian Gulf. Some people like to call it the Arabian Gulf.

Abla Amina: What are the land and climate like in Southwest Asia?

Muhammad: The Arabian Peninsula is almost all desert. Land around the edges gets some rain. There are mountains on three sides, and some in the middle of the desert. The land is flatter along the Persian Gulf.

Omar: The Arabian Peninsula is separated from the rest of Asia by three bodies of water. They are the Mediterranean Sea, the Persian Gulf and two rivers, called the Tigris and Euphrates. The rivers

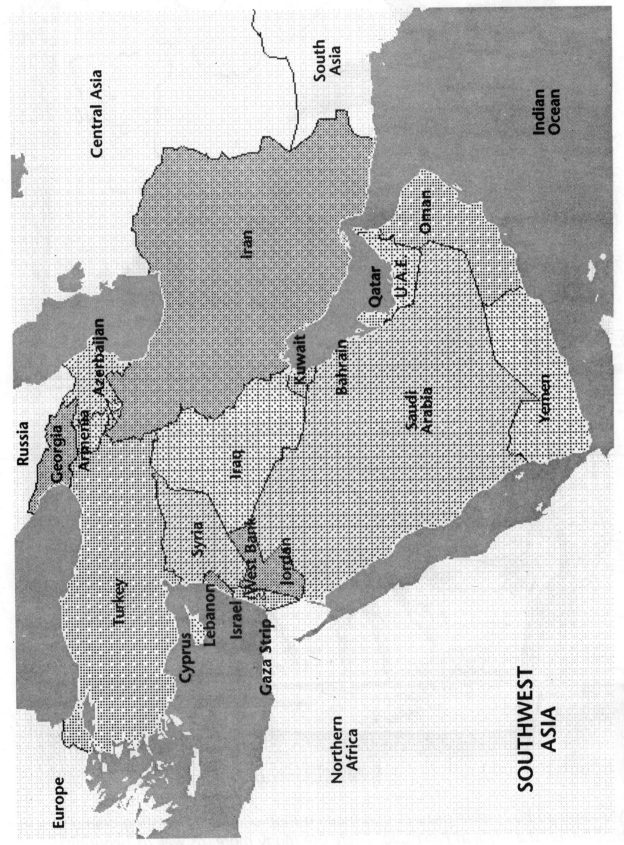

Map of Southwest Asia

Muhammad has drawn pictures and made a map of some interesting animals that live on the Arabian Peninsula. There are many more, as well as beautiful plants, trees and landscapes.

and the seacoast form a shape like a crescent moon. The land along this crescent is very good farmland. It is called the **Fertile Crescent**. People have farmed there for thousands of years. It is also the land of many prophets, like Ibrahim, Yusuf, Dawud, Sulaiman and Issa.

Nada (Turkey): Prophet Muhammad ﷺ was born in the Arabian Peninsula, in Makkah.

Muhammad: In Oman, where we come from, and in Yemen, there are also some farmlands. It doesn't rain much, though. I drew a picture of an animal that is found in Arabia. It is called an ORYX. We also drew a picture of a snake, and a camel and rider and some birds. These are some of the unusual animals that live in Arabia.

Nada: The other parts of Southwest Asia are nearly all mountains. In between the mountains are deserts. Turkey is on a peninsula called Asia Minor. That means "little" Asia. It has mountains, rivers and farmlands. It rains there in the winter, but not much in summer. The biggest river is the Euphrates. There are many smaller rivers and some large and small lakes.

Omar: Between the Caspian and the Black Seas, there is a line of mountains. It is called the Caucasus. Mountains stretch down all the way through the eastern part of Iraq and into Iran.

Abla Amina: You did a good job on a difficult geography subject. Thank you. Now we will look at Central Asia.

Central Asia

Burhan (Uzbekistan): Nur and I studied the part of the world from which our families came. It is a large region that contains many new countries. They used to be part of a large country called the Soviet Union. Now they are six **independent** countries.

Nur (China): The part of Central Asia that I come from is still part of China. It is not independent. It is a region called Xinjiang.

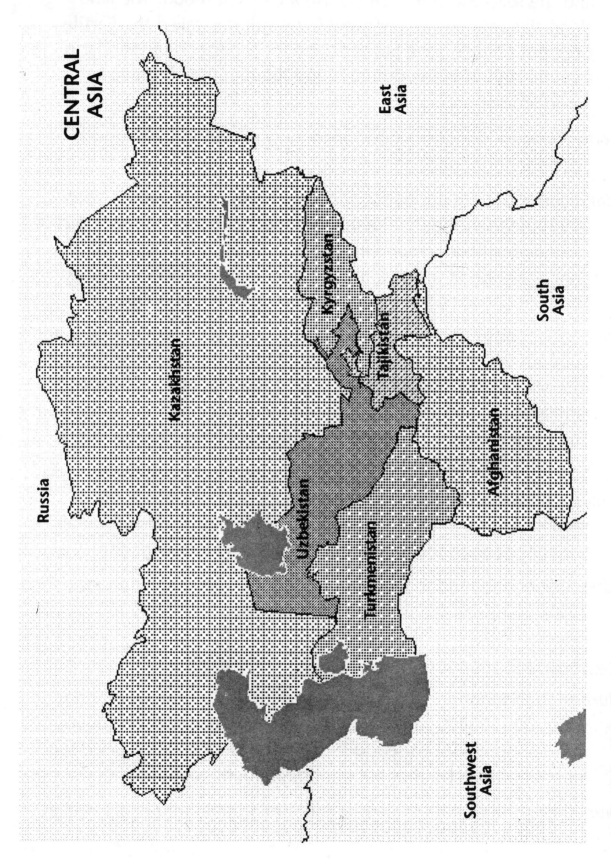

Map of Central Asia

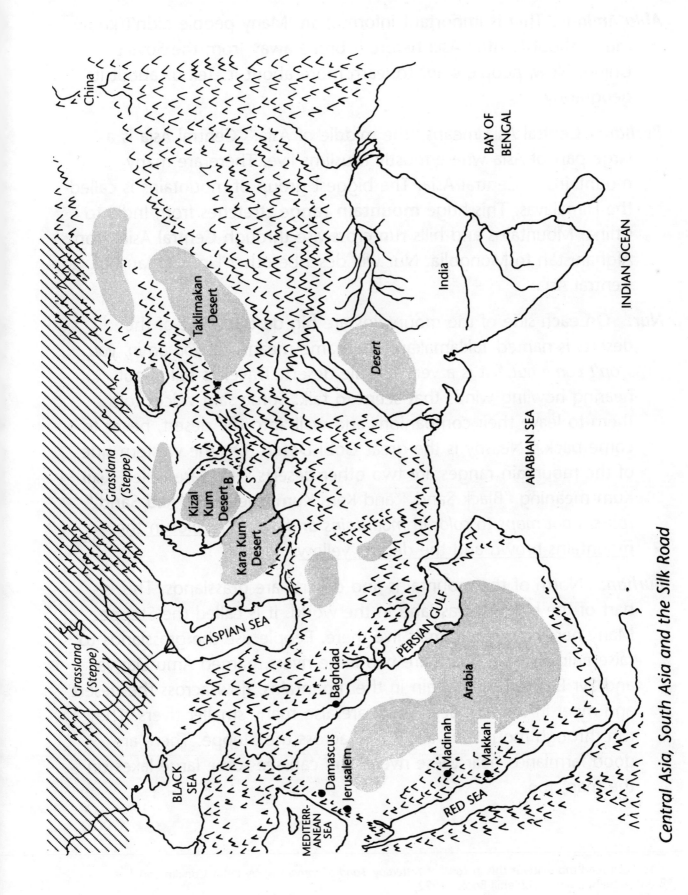

Central Asia, South Asia and the Silk Road

Abla Amina: That is important information. Many people didn't know much about Central Asia before it broke away from the Soviet Union. Now, people want to learn more about it. Tell us about its geography.

Burhan: Central Asia means "the middle of Asia." Central Asia is a large part of Asia where mostly Muslims live. There are many mountains in Central Asia. The biggest group of mountains is called the Himalayas. This huge **mountain range** stretches from India to China. Mountains and hills run crosswise through Central Asia, from Afghanistan to Mongolia. Nur will describe other kinds of land in Central Asia.

Nur: On each side of the mountains are big deserts. One of the deserts is named Taklamakan. The name means, *"If you go in, you won't come out."* It is a very terrible desert. Travelers tell about hearing howling winds that seem to talk. Some said voices told them to leave their companions and walk into the desert, never to come back.✩ Nearby is the great Gobi Desert. On the western side of the mountain ranges are two other deserts. They are called Kizil Kum meaning "Black Sand," and Kara Kum, meaning "Red Sand." *[passes out maps to color in mountains and deserts]* <u>Color in the mountains brown and the deserts yellow</u>.

Burhan: North of the mountains and deserts are grasslands. This is part of the biggest grassland in the world. It is called the Steppe. Many herds of wild animals live there. People use the grasslands to raise animals, too. There are two large rivers, named Amu Dar'ya and Syr Dar'ya. They begin in the mountains, flow across the desert and meet in the Aral Sea. There are also many smaller rivers. They run through mountain valleys and across the Steppe. There are good farmlands near these rivers. You can see some large lakes on the map, too.

✩ You can read more about this in *Land of Yesterday, Land of Tomorrow,* by Peter Conklin and Brent Aschebranner (Cobblehill Books, 1992).

Abla Amina: Thank you for bringing in the maps. Please, everyone, <u>color in the Steppe in light green, and the rivers and lakes in blue</u>.

South and Southeast Asia

Abla Amina: The last Muslim region we will study is Southern Asia. You will see that it has very different geography from the regions we have studied so far.

Nabil (Pakistan):   We studied a part of Asia where many, many Muslims live. There are a few Muslim countries, but in most parts, Muslims live mixed with other groups of people.

Sayyid (Kashmir):   Our part of Asia is divided into two parts, South Asia and Southeast Asia. South Asia is a large peninsula shaped like an upside-down triangle. One country, called India, covers most of the peninsula. The peninsula of South Asia sticks out into the Indian Ocean. To the west is the Arabian Sea. To the east is a large body of water called the Bay of Bengal. The peninsula has many different kinds of **landforms**. There are hills and flat land. There are many rivers and valleys. There are some mountains, too.

Nabil: In northern part of the peninsula, the Himalayan mountains and the Hindu Kush mountains begin. Kashmir and Pakistan are two places where most of the people are Muslims. Many Muslims live in India, too.

Sayyid: That's true, Nabil. Much of Pakistan and all of Kashmir are in the mountains. Two large rivers begin in these mountains. The Indus River flows through Pakistan and part of India. It empties into the Arabian Sea. The Ganges River flows east into the Bay of Bengal. At the mouth of the Ganges River is a small country called Bangladesh. All along the rivers are important farmlands. Farmers there grow food for their people. In most of South Asia, it rains a lot for part of the year and it is dry part of the year.

Abla Amina: Let's color our maps to help us find the places that Nabil and Sayyid described. <u>Color the South Asian peninsula red</u>.

SOUTH ASIA

East Asia

Southeast Asia

Bhutan

Bangladesh

Nepal

India

Sri Lanka

Central Asia

Pakistan

Maldives

Southwest Asia

Indian Ocean

Map of South Asia

Remember its triangle shape. <u>Color the mountains brown</u>. <u>Use blue to color the Arabian Sea, the Indian Ocean and the Bay of Bengal</u>. *[The students color their maps.]* Now, let's hear about Southeast Asia.

Ibrahim (Indonesia): Southeast Asia is made up of another peninsula and some islands in the Indian Ocean. To find Southeast Asia, look east across the Bay of Bengal from India. There are many countries in Southeast Asia. There are three Muslim countries in Southeast Asia. They are Malaysia, Indonesia and Brunei.

Nabil: Most of Southeast Asia has a **tropical wet** climate. That means the weather is usually hot and rainy. These places have some of the world's rain forests. A lot of Southeast Asia's land is hills and mountains. There are many rivers. Around the coasts are flat lands. Off the coast are thousands of islands.

Ibrahim: The largest group of islands is my country, Indonesia. In the rain forests are lots of unusual animals and plants. Tigers, elephants, dragon lizards and even rhinos live on the islands. There is a kind of ape called orangutan. In Malay language, the name means "man of the forest." There is a giant flower as big as a dinner table. It is red and smells like rotten meat. The bugs love it, though.

Abla Amina: Thanks for those interesting facts, Ibrahim. Indonesia also has the largest Muslim population of any country in the world.

Ibrahim: Brunei is another Muslim country on one of Southeast Asia's islands. The Philippines is also a country where many Muslims live. The Philippines is a group of large islands east of Indonesia. Many Muslims also live in the Maldives, a group of tiny islands near the west coast of India.

Abla Amina: Now we have looked at some of the places in the world where most of the Muslims live. In many of those places, Muslims live as the **majority**. That means the number of Muslims is larger than the number of people in any other group. In some other countries, Muslims live grouped together in certain parts of the country as a majority. These are called Muslim regions. For

Map of Southeast Asia

example, many Muslims live in western China. Nur's parents came from that part of China. It is called Xinjiang.

In countries like the United States, France and Great Britain, Muslims live as a **minority**. A minority is less than half of the total population of a country. Remember, we learned from the *Map of the Muslim World* that minorities can be large or small. Now, Zaid and Amele will tell us about some parts of the world where Muslims live as minorities.

Other Regions: Europe and the Americas

Amele (Bosnia): We studied Europe first. Europe is called a continent, but it is really attached to Asia. Europe is a huge peninsula on the western edge of Asia. West of Europe is the Atlantic Ocean. Europe is north of Africa. There are only two Muslim countries in Europe— Albania and my country, Bosnia. Other countries with large Muslim minorities are nearby. Bulgaria, Romania and Macedonia are three examples. Many Muslims also live in France, Germany, Italy and England.

Abla Amina: Spain and Portugal used to be a Muslim country called Andalusia long ago.

Zaid (U.S.): I studied countries in North and South America where many Muslims live. There are only three countries where more than 1 out of 10 people are Muslim. Trinidad is an island country in the Caribbean Sea. The other two countries are Guyana and Surinam. They are in South America, near the Caribbean Sea. I wonder why so many Muslims live there!

Abla Amina: When you study history, you will find out. They were brought there to work.

Zaid: Argentina and the U.S. are two other countries with large Muslim minorities. Muslims in Argentina and the U.S. live mostly in cities.

Abla Amina: Thank you, class. You did a great job working with the maps.

Map of Europe

Thinking About Section 3:

1. Physical maps show mountains, _____, _____ and _____.

2. Name 3 rivers in Africa and 2 in Asia.

3. Name the bodies of water that surround the Arabian Peninsula.

4. List 5 Muslim countries that are nearly all desert.

5. List 3 Muslim countries that are very mountainous.

Thinking a little harder . . .

Write a paragraph about the land and climate in Muslim lands. In a few sentences, describe what you learned from the students' reports.

USING RESOURCES IN PLACES WHERE MUSLIMS LIVE

Abla Amina: Let's look at what we have learned. What do we know, and what don't we know yet?

Zaid: First, we learned which countries have mostly Muslim populations. There, Muslims are the **majority**. We found out where those countries are located.

Khadija: We also saw where large groups of Muslims live in other countries where most people are not Muslim. They are the **minority**.

Amele: In our groups, we studied the way the land looks in the countries where many Muslims live.

Abla Amina: Fine. Now, what don't we know? What do we still need to learn about?

Nur: I've got it! We know where they live, but we don't know how they live. What kind of houses do they live in? What kind of clothes do they wear?

Khadija: We don't know what kinds of food they eat.

Muhammad: What kind of jobs do the people have?

Abla Amina: Good ideas! You are talking about things that people use. Anything that people use to help them live is called a **resource**. Where do resources come from?

Omar: The Qur'an teaches Muslims that Allah (SWT) gives people everything that we need.

Nabil: Yes! Allah (SWT) gives us trees and stones for building houses.

These students in Abla Amina's class are making models of homes and other buildings in Muslim regions. The one with the pointed roofs is from Indonesia. The one with the half-round dome is from northern Africa. The tall apartment building might be found in many cities in the world. The one in the background is from Turkey or eastern Europe.

Omar: Some people live in tents. A few people, like the Bedouin in my country, don't live in one place at all. They move about with their animals. They live in tents.

Nur: In Central Asia, there are some people like that. They live in houses made out of wool felt, called *yurts*. When it's time to move, they fold up their houses. They keep horses, sheep and sometimes camels with two humps.

Fatima: In Algeria there are people like that, too. They know how to live in the desert. They are called Berbers. They keep camels and travel across the Sahara Desert. We are from a city in Algeria. Some of our friends are Berbers. But they have moved to the city. They live in houses made of bricks and cement, just like here.

Abla Amina: You seem to have the idea! I think some of you might enjoy building models of different kinds of houses from Muslim regions. Other groups can look up more information about resources.

STUDENT NARRATOR: For the rest of the project, we used even more kinds of maps. We used books from the library. We used the encyclopedia sets in the library, and we used the CD-ROM encyclopedia on the computer. We interviewed our parents. We took notes of what we were learning. We made models and drew pictures. We hope you like our reports.

[After one week . . .]

Abla Amina: You have been working for several days on your research projects and models. You have done a very nice job. I see that you have large and small model buildings. Where are these different homes found?

Khadija: Some are found in cities. Some are found in the countryside.

Abla Amina: In the classroom atlas, there is a chart that shows whether more people live in cities or countryside. It looks like this:

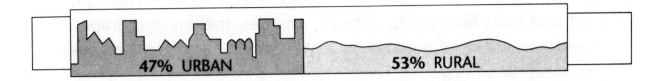

47% URBAN   53% RURAL

If you study the charts for Muslim regions, you will see that about half of the people in Muslim regions live in cities, and about half in the countryside. Places where cities are located are called **urban**. Land outside of cities is called **rural**. What do people in rural places do?

Rahma: Many people in the countryside are farmers. They grow crops of all kinds. They raise animals.

Abla Amina: Farming is important for growing food in most countries. Which group of students has information on farming? What did you learn about the resources that farmers use?

Using Resources in Rural Places

Khadija: We learned that farmers use resources and produce resources. They use land and water and seeds, and they produce crops and other things. People eat the food they produce, and people make things out of some crops, too.

Rahma: We found out that there are different ways to farm. In some places it rains enough. In other places, it rains only a few months each year. In many places where Muslims live, farmers have to water their own crops. That is called **irrigation**. We found pictures of different kinds of irrigation. Farmers use animals and machines.

Abla Amina: What important crops did you learn about?

Sayyid: We looked at a picture atlas. It showed pictures of the crops and animals that farmers produce. In Muslim countries of Asia, we found cotton, rubber trees, pepper, coconuts, tea, coffee, and rice. Jute fiber makes ropes and sacks that are used all over the world. Vegetable oil comes from olives, palms and sunflowers.

Burhan: People in Central Asia grow a lot of cotton, too. They grow nuts and fruits like apples, apricots, cherries, melons and grapes. We saw a picture of a house for drying raisins. Important animals are sheep and horses.

Sayyid: In Kashmir, Mongolia and China, they raise a special kind of sheep with very soft wool.

Abla Amina: They make it into cashmere sweaters. I have a nice one.

Muhammad: In Arabia, farmers raise wheat in the desert, and even flowers. Dates are an important crop in many Arab countries.

Omar: In Palestine, they grow olives, oranges, lemons and limes.

Fatima: In North Africa they grow olives and citrus fruits like those, too. Moroccan farmers grow fruits and vegetables. In West Africa, people grow lots of peanuts and cotton.

Omar: In Iran, Turkey and Lebanon, people raise silkworms to make silk cloth from the cocoons.

Muhammad: Omani people gather incense from a desert tree. It burns with a nice perfume.

Ali: In Yemen and East Africa, people grow coffee. Other important crops from Africa are tea, vanilla, cloves and cacao beans, for chocolate. Sugar cane, dates, coconuts, pineapples and bananas, oranges and lemons make a good dessert from Africa. After dinner, chew some gum. Most of the **gum** in the world's bubble gum comes from Sudan.

Khadija: In all of those places, people raise food crops that they use for themselves. They sell the fancy products to people in other countries. In places where the land is too dry for farms, they raise animals for meat, milk, wool and leather.

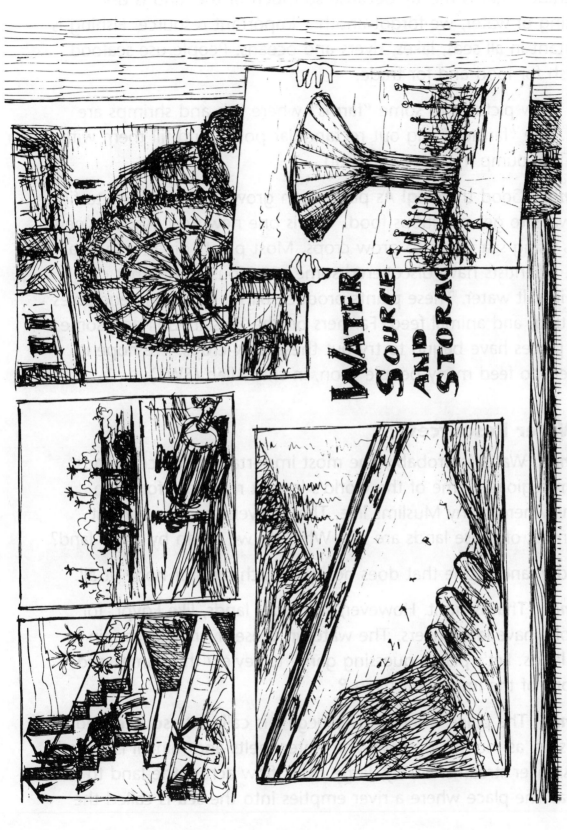

Some students in the class found pictures in library books and magazines. They made posters showing different ways of storing and using water. On the top row, the picture on the left shows a well in the Sahara Desert. The middle poster shows two ways of pumping irrigation water to crops: an animal and a motor. The large poster shows a very old, wooden water wheel in Syria. It is still working after hundreds of years. The two pictures in the first row show a modern dam and water tower.

Abla Amina: Some Muslim countries do not grow enough food, so they trade. That is mostly because so much of the land is dry. Speaking of water, we forgot another important resource. Fishing is important in all seas, lakes, rivers and oceans. People use seafood and fish for food and for trade.

Rahma: I saw pictures of some "farms" where fish and shrimps are raised. The "farmers" dig out rectangular ponds and fill them with fish. They pump in water and food.

Abla Amina: Good thinking! As population grows, people need to find new ways to get nutritious food. This is one new way. Another new way is using sea water to grow crops. Most plants die in salty sea water. Scientists have discovered some nutritious plants that can grow in salt water. These plants produce oil for cooking, vegetables for eating, and animal feed. Farmers on the Persian Gulf and some other places have begun to try out these new crops. We hope it can help to feed many people soon, in sha' Allah (SWT).

Using Water Resources

Abla Amina: Water is probably the most important resource in most Muslim regions. Some of the world's largest rivers are found in regions where many Muslims live. That is even more important since most of those lands are dry. What do we mean by a dry land?

Zaid: A dry land is one that does not get much rain, or none at all.

Abla Amina: That is right. However, some dry lands, like Egypt, for example, have large rivers. The water in these rivers falls as rain in other lands. Let's play a guessing game to review the names and locations of the important rivers.°

Abla Amina: The place where a river begins is called its **source**. Most rivers start as mountain snow. The water melts and rainfall is added from smaller streams. Finally, large rivers flow across the land to the sea. The place where a river empties into the sea is called the

---

° See Worksheet #4.

mouth. At the mouth, a river fans out as it empties into the sea. Who knows what sometimes forms at the mouth of large rivers?

Anas: I know that one! The river drops a lot of soil, and it makes a *delta*. A delta is a triangle of rich soil. The Nile delta, where my father was born, has many farms and villages.

Abla Amina: That's right. Many rivers have deltas. Can you name some important deltas? In which countries are they located?

Nabil: The Ganges delta covers most of Bangladesh, and the Indus delta is in Pakistan.

Rahma: The Niger River in Africa has two deltas. One is in the middle, where the river bends, in Mali. The other one is at the mouth, in Nigeria.

Burhan: The Amu Dar'ya and Syr Dar'ya have deltas. They empty into the Aral Sea in Uzbekistan. But now the Aral Sea is drying up. People take out too much water for farming and cities. This is a big problem in Uzbekistan and nearby countries.

Zaid: Why is that a problem?

Nur: We read about it in some library books. Fishing boats that used to be in the water are stuck on dry land. There are hardly any more fish. Salt from the sea dries up and blows all over farm land. That is bad for crops and people.

Abla Amina: We began to talk about irrigation and other ways to use water. You drew some posters for the bulletin board. Who would like to start explaining the pictures?

Omar: I will, in sha' Allah. I worked with Zaid, Nabil, Nur and Nada. Farmers irrigate their crops when there isn't enough rain. That means they bring water from a river, or from underground. A long time ago, most Muslim farmers used animals hooked to water wheels to raise water. Sometimes people even did the work. Now, people mostly use motors to pump water. Anas drew us a picture of the ones he saw in Egypt.

Zaid: Sometimes people made ditches or canals to bring the water down by gravity. Nur and I drew a picture of a kind of pipe that brings water from the mountains. It's called a **qanat**.

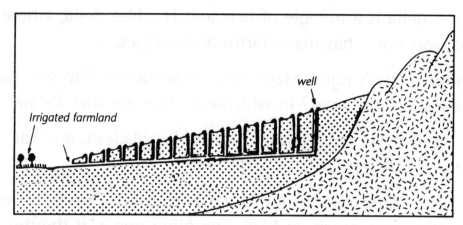

Qanat Irrigation

Nur: They use it in China, Iran and North Africa. Many people have to work together to build it and keep it working. Workers dig a small tunnel underground from the mountain to the fields. All along the tunnel they dig holes to the top. Some of the holes are so small that only children can fit inside! The water runs to the fields by itself. It doesn't need a pump.

Zaid: The water stays underground all the way. The sun can't evaporate it. The hard part is keeping the tunnel open. It gets filled with mud, and sometimes it collapses. People work hard to keep the qanat open.

Abla Amina: What is the striped tower in the picture?

Nabil: That is a water tower, a huge tank. Many cities in Arabia use them to store water. This one is in Riyadh. In Kuwait, they have many together. They look like flowers in a vase. They use it to store water for the city. They also have reservoirs. A reservoir is a man-made lake.

Omar: The tanks are also used to store sea water. In Saudi Arabia, they make most of their water by taking the salt out of sea water. That takes a lot of energy, but they use their own oil and gas, so it's not expensive.

Nada: I drew a picture of the **dam**. A dam is a huge wall built to hold back a river. When they close the dam, a lake fills up behind it. I read about a project to build a big dam in Turkey. It is called the Ataturk Dam. It holds back the Euphrates River.

Abla Amina: What does a dam do?

Nada: People store water behind a dam. They let the water out when they need it. Farms and cities use the water.

Omar: It can keep a river from flooding too much. Another big dam is in Egypt. It holds back the Nile River. Many other rivers have dams. Syria has another dam on the Euphrates River, but it is not as big as the one in Turkey.

Nabil: You can also make electricity with a dam. When the water goes through the dam, it turns big wheels hooked up to generators. We couldn't draw those—it was too hard. Anyway, the electricity goes on wires to people all over the country.

Abla Amina: Dams are very important for a country. They are also very expensive to build. Do they cause any problems?

Nada: Our book said that different countries have problems sharing water. When you hold it back, not so much is left in the river. Farmers also take a lot of the water.

Burhan: That's what happened to the Aral Sea! There isn't enough water left to fill it!

Abla Amina: I read once that very little water actually reaches the sea from the Nile. People use almost all of it before it gets to the river's mouth.

Nur: We read about crops grown in the middle of the desert, in big, round fields. People drill for water deep underground. They pump it into sprinkler pipes that turn around and around. Other crops are grown by dripping water on the roots from plastic tubes, drop by drop.

Abla Amina: That's right. They do that to save precious water in dry countries. Underground water is like gold. Allah (SWT) made underground lakes and rivers. It is mentioned in the Qur'an. ✶ When people use it up, it is gone, it will take a long time for it to fill again. Water may never fill those underground spaces again. A big problem for Muslim countries and all others, too, is pollution. Big cities, farming and factories put chemicals and waste into seas and rivers.

Underground Resources

Abla Amina: Let us look at another kind of resource now. We just learned how farmers work hard to raise food and other products. We learned how people work hard to get water for many uses, even from underground. Who studied resources that Allah (SWT) placed underground as a blessing for Muslims?

Petroleum and Natural Gas

Ibrahim: An important resource we found in many Muslim countries is oil, sometimes called **petroleum**. Many countries that have oil also have **natural gas**.

Abla Amina: Why are petroleum and natural gas so important?

Ibrahim: Everyone in the world needs **energy**. Oil is made into gasoline for cars and trucks, fuel for trains and airplanes, and for all kinds of motors. They use it to heat houses and schools and for running factories. Gas is used for cooking and heating, and for making electricity for homes and factories.

Amele: Another important use for oil is making plastic. Toys, bags, computers, cars, and millions of things are made with plastics. Even medicines and other chemicals use oil.

✶ ". . . Or the water of the garden will run off underground so that you will not be able to find it." (Qur'an 18:41)

"And we send life-giving winds then cause the rain to descend from the sky, providing you with water in plenty, though you are not the guardians of its stores." (Qur'an 15:22)

Fatima: Oil makes a country very rich when they have lots of it. The people in the country use what they have, and they sell it to other countries.

Sayyid: Oil from Muslim countries around the Persian Gulf is sent all over the world. More oil is found there than in any other part of the world.

Fatima: North African countries have oil, too, like Algeria, Tunisia and Libya.

Sayyid: Other countries with oil and gas are the new countries in Central Asia, and Nigeria, Indonesia and Albania, a country in Europe.

Abla Amina: Allah (SWT) granted a generous blessing to the Muslim countries in this way. But every blessing comes with a responsibility. What can Muslims do with this money to help people in the world?

Amele: They use money from selling oil to help build the country. With the money they earn from selling it, they have built schools, hospitals and factories. Some of the money from oil helps to print books and make videos about Islam to send to other countries. Muslim countries should also use some money to help poor people.

Abla Amina: Are there any disadvantages to having oil and other rich resources?

Sayyid: Oil can make pollution. Oil puts smog in the air when burned. It spills out of wells and ships into water. Chemicals from oil can get into soil and water to cause problems. Some people have been careless. They can't always control it. When it accidentally spills into water, animals and fish die. Even when there isn't a big accident, ships that carry oil sometimes spill some.

Muhammad: In the Persian Gulf, they used to find pearls, but now that business is not doing very well. Fishing is still important, but that business is in danger, too.

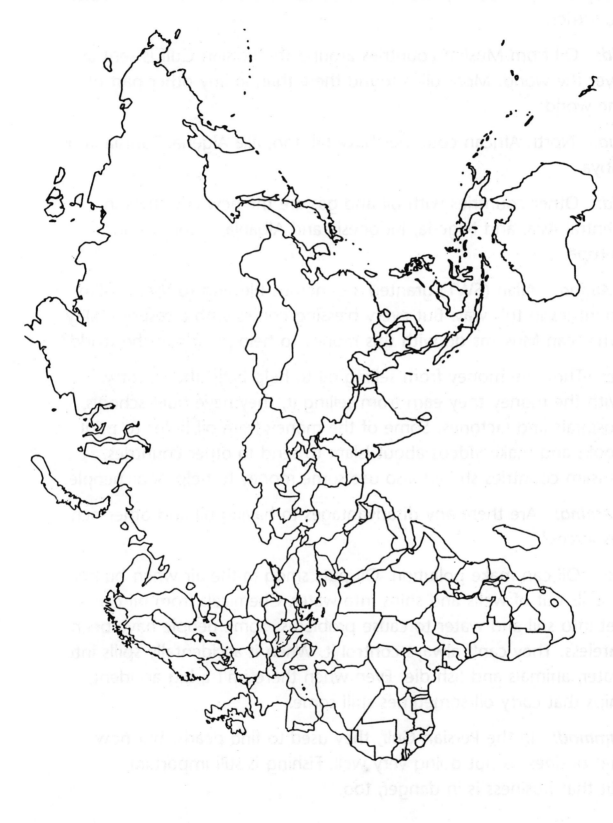

Use an encyclopedia or atlas and the pictographs on Worksheet #7 to locate important underground resources in Muslim countries.

Abla Amina: There is another problem I want to mention. What are these countries going to do when the oil is gone? What will they have left to sell? Many oil-producing countries are trying to build factories and start many kinds of work to keep people working when there is no more oil. They are also trying to save some of the money. They also put money into banks and other businesses.

There is another way to use oil to make more money. Instead of selling it just as it comes out of the ground, they keep it and make things out of it, like plastics and chemicals. These can be sold for more money than oil just as it comes out of the ground.

In some countries, the oil is already starting to run out. In other Muslim regions, like Central Asia, they are just starting to bring it out of the ground. Those countries will see many changes in the years ahead.

Using Resources in Urban Places

Abla Amina: We just heard Sayyid, Fatima and Amele tell us all about oil. They told us that most of it is loaded into ships for transport to other countries. Some of the oil is used at home. Ibrahim made a map with symbols for other minerals found in Muslim countries.°
Many of those minerals are transported to other countries, too. Many leaders in these countries want to find ways to make products from these resources. Then they want to sell finished products to others. These products would be made in factories. The factories are mostly in **urban** places, in cities. They would provide jobs for many urban workers. Which group studied factory work and products?

Factories Make Many Different Products

Omar: We had to learn a new word when we tried to look up this information. We found out that a group of factories making products is called an **industry**. We found a list of the **industries** for each Muslim country in the encyclopedia.

° Use Worksheet #7 and an encyclopedia or resource atlas to make your own map of these resources.

Anas: Then we noticed that almost all of the countries had the same kinds of factories. It got boring to write them all down.

Abla Amina: So what did you do? How did you solve the problem?

Anas: We asked the computer teacher to help us make a list. She showed us how to use software to make a database. We listed all of the industries at the top, and the countries down the side. We just checked the boxes for each industry in the country. You can see our list on the bulletin board. We printed it out from the computer.

Abla Amina: Who can tell us what those factories and industries make?

Omar: Most of the countries make **textiles**. That means the factories weave and knit cloth, or sew it into clothes. Many countries make shoes. Many make cement. Some have factories for making medicines.

Factories that process food are important in farming countries. **Processing** means making food into grocery store products. For example, if you grow tomatoes, the factory makes tomato sauce. Countries that grow fruit make juice, jelly and canned or dried fruit. Peanuts turn into peanut oil, peanut butter, and animal feed.

Anas: Fewer countries make cars, trucks and machines, or things like washing machines and refrigerators. Wood pulp and paper are made from forest lands.*

Abla Amina: Who buys the goods made in these industries? What kind of goods are they?

Anas: People living in these countries need to buy clothes, shoes, refrigerators and things like that. People who build things need other goods. Almost all of the big countries have cement factories. Many of them make iron and steel, and some machines. Bigger countries have factories for cars and trucks, or farm machines. They sell some of them to nearby countries.

---

* Guess which countries have forest products and paper industries? Hint—go to section 3.

INDUSTRIES IN MUSLIM COUNTRIES

COUNTRY	Textiles	Food Processing	Oil Refining	Metals	Fertilizer	Chemicals	Paper	Machinery	Electronics	Consumer Goods	Cement
ALBANIA	✓	✓	✓	✓	✓		✓	✓		✓	✓
ALGERIA	✓	✓	✓	✓	✓	✓				✓	
AZERBAIJAN	✓	✓	✓	✓		✓					✓
BAHRAIN	✓		✓	✓	✓	✓					
BANGLADESH	✓										
BOSNIA-HERZ.											
BRUNEI			✓								
CHAD		✓									
DJIBOUTI		✓				✓				✓	✓
EGYPT	✓	✓		✓	✓	✓				✓	✓
ERITREA		✓									
GAMBIA	✓	✓									
INDONESIA	✓	✓	✓	✓	✓	✓	✓			✓	✓
IRAN	✓	✓	✓	✓	✓	✓		✓	✓	✓	✓
JORDAN	✓	✓	✓	✓	✓	✓	✓			✓	✓
KAZAKHSTAN	✓	✓	✓	✓	✓	✓				✓	
KUWAIT		✓	✓	✓	✓	✓				✓	
KYRGYZSTAN	✓	✓	✓		✓	✓	✓			✓	
LEBANON	✓	✓	✓	✓	✓	✓			✓	✓	✓
LIBYA	✓	✓	✓	✓		✓				✓	
MALAYSIA	✓	✓	✓		✓	✓		✓	✓	✓	✓
MALDIVES		✓									
MALI		✓									
MAURITANIA	✓	✓	✓	✓	✓	✓				✓	
MOROCCO	✓	✓	✓		✓	✓	✓	✓		✓	
NIGERIA	✓	✓	✓	✓	✓	✓		✓	✓	✓	
OMAN		✓	✓		✓			✓		✓	
PAKISTAN	✓	✓	✓		✓	✓		✓		✓	✓
QATAR		✓	✓	✓	✓	✓		✓		✓	✓
SAUDI ARABIA		✓	✓	✓	✓	✓					
SENEGAL	✓	✓	✓		✓	✓			✓	✓	
SOMALIA	✓	✓		✓		✓					
SUDAN	✓	✓				✓		✓			
SYRIA	✓	✓	✓	✓	✓	✓				✓	✓
TAJIKSTAN	✓	✓	✓	✓	✓	✓	✓	✓	✓	✓	
TUNISIA	✓	✓	✓	✓	✓	✓	✓	✓	✓	✓	
TURKEY	✓	✓	✓	✓	✓	✓		✓	✓	✓	
TURKMENISTAN	✓	✓	✓	✓	✓	✓					
U.A.R.	✓	✓	✓	✓	✓	✓		✓			
UZBEKISTAN	✓	✓									
YEMEN	✓	✓									

Omar and Anas made this chart to make it easier to list industries in Muslim countries. They made it on the computer's database program. Which five countries have the most industries? Find those countries on the map.

COUNTRY	oil	natural gas	coal	copper	chromium	nickel	iron	zinc	manganese	tungsten	silver	gold	lead	uranium	bauxite	tin	salt	potash	phosphates	gypsum	sulfur	mica	silica
AFGHANISTAN	●	●	●	○													❖						
ALBANIA	●●	●		○	○	○																	
ALGERIA	●●	●		○			○	○		○	○								❖				
AZERBAIJAN	●●	●		○			○	○					○		○		❖						
BAHRAIN	●●	●																					
BANGLADESH		●															❖						
BOSNIA-HERZ.			●				○								○								
BRUNEI	●●	●																					
CHAD	●●	●												○									
DJIBOUTI																				❖	❖	❖	
EGYPT	●●	●		○			○	○	○		○	○		○					❖				❖
ERITREA				○								○						❖					
GAMBIA																○							
GUINEA-BISSAU															○				❖				
INDONESIA	●●	●	●●	○	○	○	○		○			○			○	○							
IRAN	●	●	●	○○	○		○	○	○				○		○					❖			
IRAQ	●●●	●	●	○			○																
JORDAN							○											❖	❖				
KAZAKHSTAN	●●	●	●	○	○		○	○		○	○	○						❖					
KUWAIT	●●	●					○										❖						
KYRGYZSTAN	●		●				○							○		○							
LEBANON			●				○																
LIBYA	●●	●					○																
MALAYSIA	●●	●		○			○	○				○			○	○	❖			❖	❖		
MALDIVES																							
MALI							○					○			○		❖						
MAURITANIA	●			○			○					○							❖	❖			
MOROCCO		●	●●●	○			○	○					○				❖		❖❖❖	❖			
NIGER		●	●●				○							○					❖	❖			
NIGERIA	●●●	●●	●		○		○	○		○			○	○	○	○	❖			❖			
OMAN	●●●	●●●		○	○							○					❖			❖❖			
PAKISTAN	●	●●	●								○	○		○	○					❖			❖
QATAR	●●●	●																					
SAUDI ARABIA	●●●	●●									○	○					❖❖		❖	❖			
SENEGAL		●		○	○		○					○		○			❖			❖			
SOMALIA		●●		○			○	○	○						○		❖❖		❖	❖		❖	
SUDAN	●	●		○			○			○		○					❖			❖			
SYRIA	●●	●		○			○	○					○○	○			❖❖❖						
TAJIKSTAN		●						○			○	○	○○	○									
TUNISIA	●●	●						○								○	❖		❖				
TURKEY	●	●	●	○	○○○			○		○		○		○	○								
TURKMENISTAN	●	●●																					
U.A.R.	●	●●		○																			❖
UZBEKISTAN	●	●●●	●	○				○				○○	○	○	○				❖	❖❖			
YEMEN	●●	●					○	○		○		○○	○				❖						

● = fuels   ○ = metals   ❖ = minerals (3 symbols means world's largest producer)

Anas: Egypt makes lots of cotton thread and cloth, like towels, that go to other countries. They make lots of clothes, too.

Omar: Sometimes it is hard to tell what they make. The encyclopedia called them just *"consumer goods."*

Abla Amina: What is a **consumer**?

Khadija: A **consumer** is someone who buys things to use. Consumer goods must be things that people use in everyday life.

Abla Amina: Good, Khadija. They are things people buy for their homes and families. Other kinds of goods are used to make things, like tractors and trucks, that carry products. Machines help to make other things, too. Cement is used to make roads, buildings and houses. It is very important.

Omar: There was another kind of factory listed in the encyclopedia. It said that many countries make **export goods**. What does that mean?

Abla Amina: That means the workers make things to send out of the country after they are made. Often, the parts come from outside the country, too. Workers in the factories put them together and ship them out. If you look at the labels in clothing, you will often see "Made in Country XXX". Many companies send cloth, thread and patterns to another country and have it cut and sewn there. In Malaysia, many young women work in factories making computers, televisions and other electronics, like video games. Many products have parts made and put together in several countries.

Anas: Some other factories depend on resources, but they don't make goods that we can buy. They process resources like minerals or oil. The countries with oil refine it into gasoline, chemicals, plastic and other things. Some places have minerals for fertilizer. Many countries that have iron ore make it into steel.

Thinking About Section 4:

1. Why is water the most important resource in many Muslim regions?

2. Name some important uses for water, and ways to get it.

3. List some products you use that come from each continent.

4. Make a chart of some minerals named on the map. Draw pictures of things that are made with these minerals.

5. List some **fresh** foods and **processed** foods that you ate yesterday.

6. Put a check beside the products that are consumer goods:

__cement mixer   __pair of jeans   __dump truck   __shirt

__washing machine   __computer   __television   __toy

__cement   __hospital bed   __bicycle   __tractor

__pencil

GOOD LOCATION CAN BE A RESOURCE!

Abla Amina: We have studied resources and products from the land, from underground, and from factories. These things help people to earn a living. Sometimes, however, people can earn a good living just because of their location. Maps can help us find out about some important locations. *[pointing to a world map]* What does this map show?

Rahma: It shows the countries in different colors. It has black dots and writing to show where cities are. The biggest black dots show the biggest cities.

Where Are Cities Located?

Abla Amina: Good! Let us look at the countries where we learned that Muslims are the majority. Are there many large cities in each of these countries? Can you find a lot of large, black dots?

Muhammad: Some maps only show the capital city. In most countries, that is the largest city. The map shows the capital city as a star. Most of the countries have just a few larger cities. Many smaller dots show towns or small cities.

Abla Amina: Let's divide into two groups. Group 1 will study Africa, and Group 2 will take Asia. Look for cities, and discuss what we can learn about their **location**. What seems important about the kinds of places where cities grow up? See what the map can tell you. Share your ideas with the rest of the group. Make a chart like the one on the next page.

Make a chart to organize information about cities' location. List 10 large cities in Africa, and 10 in Asia.[°]

Continent	Name of City	Nearby Geographic Features

[After some time . . .]

Abla Amina: What kinds of land have no cities?

Nur: Deserts don't have any cities. In the African Sahara there are no large cities. In Arabia there are a few cities, though, like Riyadh, Makkah and Madinah.

Muhammad: They use water from underground. Desert cities have to get water from underground wells or springs.

Sayyid: In the mountains there are no large cities, either.

Ibrahim: You can't find many cities in the rain forest, either. Too many snakes!

Abla Amina: You are right about that! In what kind of places do you find the most cities?

Omar: We found the most cities on the biggest rivers.

[°] You may use Worksheet #8 for this chart as you work with maps in an atlas.

The Muslim World Today

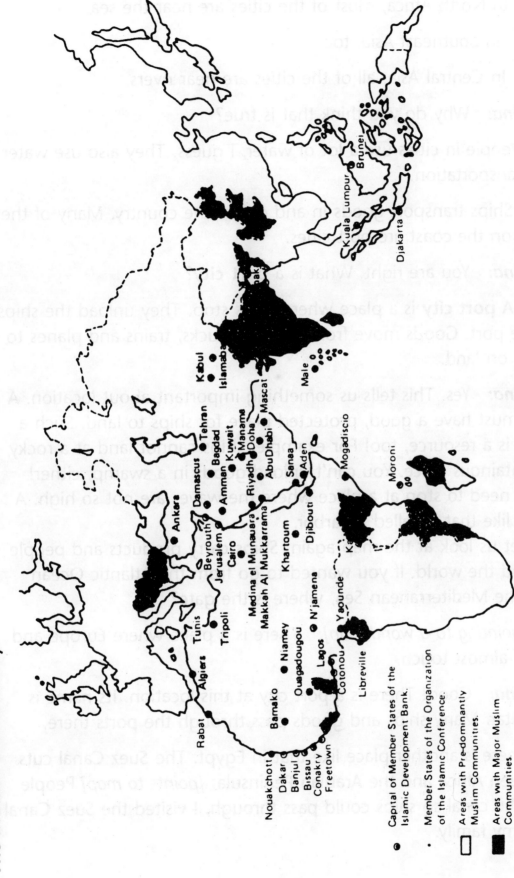

On this map, cities in Muslim regions of Asia and Africa are shown. The map was made by the Islamic Development Bank in Saudi Arabia.

Source: *The Islamic Development Bank (Jeddah, Saudi Arabia, 1986) The Eleventh Annual Report.*

Map legend:
- ● Capital of Member States of the Islamic Development Bank.
- ∙ Member States of the Organization of the Islamic Conference.
- ☐ Areas with Predominantly Muslim Communities.
- ■ Areas with Major Muslim Communities.

Cities labelled on map:
Kuala Lumpur, Brunei, Djakarta, Dakar, Kabul, Islamabad, Male, Tehran, Mascat, Damascus, Bagdad, Kuwait, Doha, AbuDhabi, Ankera, Beyrouth, Amman, Riyadh, Manama, Senaa, Mogadiscio, Jerusalem, Cairo, Medina el Munauara, Khartoum, Aden, Moroni, Makkah Al Mukkarrama, Djibouti, Tripoli, N'jamena, Yaounde, Tunis, Niamey, Lagos, Cotonou, Libreville, Algiers, Ouagadougou, Rabat, Bamako, Nouakchott, Dakar, Banjul, Bissau, Conakry, Freetown

Fatima: In North Africa, most of the cities are near the sea.

Ibrahim: In Southeast Asia, too.

Burhan: In Central Asia, all of the cities are near rivers.

Abla Amina: Why do you think that is true?

Nada: People in cities use a lot of water, I guess. They also use water for transportation.

Sayyid: Ships transport goods in and out of the country. Many of the cities on the coast are port cities.

Abla Amina: You are right. What is a **port city**?

Sayyid: A **port city** is a place where ships stop. They unload the ships in the port. Goods move from ships to trucks, trains and planes to travel on land.

Abla Amina: Yes. This tells us something important about location. A port must have a good, protected place for ships to land. Such a place is a resource, too! For example, ships cannot land at a rocky, mountainous place. You can't unload goods in a swamp, either! Ships need to stop at a place where the waves are not so high. A place like that is called a harbor.

Let us look at the map again. Ships carry products and people around the world. If you wanted to go from the Atlantic Ocean into the Mediterranean Sea, where is the gate?

Fatima [pointing to a world map]: There is a place where Europe and Africa almost touch.

Abla Amina: Good! There is a port city at this location. Its name is Gibraltar. Many ships and goods pass through the ports there.

Anas: There is another place like that in Egypt. The Suez Canal cuts between Africa and the Arabian Peninsula. [points to map] People dug the canal so ships could pass through. I visited the Suez Canal with my family.

Abla Amina: Good thinking, Anas. There are several more places like that in Muslim countries. Look at the Suez Canal. Follow the Red Sea south to its narrow end. Near it are important port cities.

Muhammad [pointing to map]: Oman, my country, is right here, at the end of the Persian Gulf. Many tankers and other ships pass by. There are many cities on the Persian Gulf.

Abla Amina: Many Arabs call it the Arabian Gulf. On one side is Iran. On the other side are Arab countries. Who can find another important location for ports?

Ibrahim: Between Indonesia and Malaysia, many ships pass on their way to and from East Asia. Singapore is an important port city where many Muslims live. It is a tiny country.

Rahma [pointing to map]: Dakar, Senegal is an important port city in Africa. It sticks right out into the sea at the widest part of Africa. It has a huge airport, too.

Abla Amina: Many important cities in Central Asia were a kind of port city long ago. Who knows about those?

Burhan: They were caravan stops. The ships were camels and horses! Samarkand and Tashkent were caravan ports.

Nada: Istanbul is a city between the Black Sea and the Mediterranean. Many ships pass by Istanbul.

Abla Amina: Very good, class! Ports are one kind of place where people earn a living mostly in **service jobs**. Service workers do things for people, like fixing, driving and supplying ships, planes or trucks. They have restaurants, hotels, markets and banks for keeping and moving money for trade. In those places, many workers can find all sorts of good jobs. **Those jobs are there because of location.**

Let's think about another kind of location. I have a riddle about a kind of place! *WHAT IS OLD AND FALLING APART, BUT MANY PEOPLE PAY MONEY TO SEE IT?*

Khadija: Why would anyone do that?

Abla Amina: I'll give you another hint. *MANY OF THEM ARE VERY LARGE, AND MADE OF STONES. MILLIONS OF PEOPLE VISIT THEM EACH YEAR.*

Omar: I know! Old buildings, like the ones in Jerusalem. People come by busloads to look at the buildings. They take photos and visit shops to buy souvenirs.

Anas: And the pyramids in Egypt! I rode a camel there once. It was very high off the ground.

Abla Amina: There are many places in Muslim countries that visitors, or **tourists**, like to see. Tourists make jobs for many people. What other kinds of places do tourists like to visit?

Fatima: They like to visit warm places when it's winter where they live. They like cool places when it's hot where they live. People from Europe come to visit the beaches in Algeria in the winter.

Abla Amina: That's a good reason to travel, if you can afford it. I have another riddle. *NAME A PLACE THAT EVERY MUSLIM WANTS TO GO.*

Nur: Makkah! They want to make hajj.

Abla Amina: Right! The people who visit Makkah are important for Saudi Arabia. They had to build roads, airports, hotels, hospitals and other buildings for millions of Muslim visitors each year. They must provide many services to take care of them during their visit. Visitors come all year long, to make *'umrah,* not just during the hajj. They bring in lots of income and make jobs. It is also a great challenge to host all those people.

Thinking About Section 5:

1. What is a port city? Why do some cities become important ports?

2. Name some places in the world that attract tourists.

3. Write about the place where you live. What is important about its location? (Ask your parents or teacher to help you find out.)

PEOPLE ARE THE MOST IMPORTANT RESOURCE FOR A COUNTRY

STUDENT NARRATOR: Abla Amina walked into the class. She wrote on the blackboard in large letters:

PEOPLE ARE IMPORTANT RESOURCES

Abla Amina: What can we add to what we know now about resources in places where Muslims live?

Zaid: How can people be a resource? I thought resources are something that people use!

Khadija: People need people, too! When you are sick, you need a doctor. We need our teacher, Abla Amina, to help us learn.

Abla Amina: Thanks, Khadija. I appreciate that. You are right. All kinds of service workers and producers are important resources for a country. In the past few days we learned about many products and natural resources. People using resources have many different jobs. Who can name some of the jobs that people living in Muslim countries do?

Nabil: Farmers, oil workers and factory workers are some jobs.

Zaid: You told us about service workers. Some of them serve tourists and other visitors. Bankers, barbers and teachers are also service workers. So are cowboys!

Nada: What about the people who build dams and reservoirs? Engineers and construction workers build all kinds of things. My uncle is an engineer.

Fatima, Nabil, Nada and Anas brought letters and photographs of their relatives. Their uncles, cousins and aunts live and work far away from them in other countries. Family members like to stay in touch, so they write letters, send photos and talk to each other on the telephone. Whenever they travel, families try to visit each other.

Ibrahim: Truck drivers, pilots and ship captains carry products to different places.

Abla Amina: Good thinking, class! People are resources! That is one reason why countries need to educate citizens. There must be enough doctors, teachers, engineers, skilled farmers, builders and other workers for thousands of different jobs. For many poor countries, it is a struggle just to make sure that everyone learns to read and write!

Zaid: Why is that so hard to do? Doesn't everyone go to school like us?

Fatima: My mother told me that some children living in the Sahara live too far from schools.

Anas: My father was a teacher in his village. He said that some children didn't do their homework. He said that they worked hard after school in the fields with their parents every day.

Nur: In one library book it said that in China, some parents are too poor to pay for school fees, clothes or books.

Workers on the Move

Abla Amina: Some countries don't have enough educated people to fill important jobs. They have to find a way to solve the problem. Let's think about two situations that might happen in a country. *[writing on the blackboard]*

Country	Jobs Problem	People Problem	Solution
#1	too many jobs	not enough people with the right skills and education	
#2	not enough jobs	too many people looking for jobs	

Abla Amina: Can anyone think of a country like #1 or #2?

Fatima: I heard my parents talking about my uncle. He couldn't find a job in Algeria. Now he lives in France.

Anas: My parents want us to move back to Egypt, but they say that it is too hard to find work there. So we still live here in the U.S.

Abla Amina: You just figured out the solution to #2! In countries that have too many people without jobs, some of the workers leave. They look for jobs in other countries.

Zaid: What if the other countries also don't have enough jobs? Do people fight over jobs?

Nada: My parents told me that many Turkish workers live in Germany. They have a hard time there. Many people want them to go back. My cousins were born in Germany. We have a hard time understanding each other. They go to school in Germany.

Nabil: We have relatives in California and New York. They come to visit us. They sit around and talk about their jobs all the time.

Abla Amina: You are doing some good thinking. These are all examples of Country #2 on the chart. Jobs are very important. People use the money from jobs to buy food, housing, and even toys for you. So, what can we write in the chart under #2: Solution?

Ibrahim: Let me try: "WORKERS FIND JOBS IN OTHER COUNTRIES."·

Fatima: There is another way. May I write it, Abla Amina? *[she nods]* "TRY TO MAKE MORE JOBS."

Abla Amina: Excellent, Fatima! That is one part of **development**. People try to build more factories and other kinds of jobs. Countries try to use resources to develop jobs and other things that the country needs. Development can bring in money, but it also costs money. Let's look at Country #1 again. Lots of oil-producing countries have this problem.

Muhammad: We read about that in our group. Oil countries need lots of workers. They need workers for the oil wells. The country gets money from selling oil. They use the money to build cities and factories and schools.

Ibrahim: So in the solution box for #1, I can write, "BRING WORKERS FROM OTHER COUNTRIES."

Abla Amina: You are terrific students! We have finished the chart. Many oil countries bring in workers from other Muslim countries. They work as teachers, doctors, office workers. They work in water stations, power plants and construction. Most of them speak Arabic. They are Muslim, and they share a way of life. Of course, they also have their differences. Many workers in oil countries are from other parts of Asia, or from Europe and the U.S. In fact, the U.S. itself has workers from many countries. That has been true for a long time. People from all over the world built U.S. cities, farms and transportation.

Sayyid: I hope I will get a good job when I grow up.

Abla Amina: To get a good job, you will need a good education. Some Muslim countries have built many schools and large universities. They also send people to other countries for training. Doctors, engineers and scientists are good examples. Such workers need to stay in touch with each other so their knowledge will be up-to-date.

Thinking About Section 6:

1. Name four kinds of service workers that help you.

2. What can governments do so that they have skilled workers in a country?

3. Think about, or talk to someone whose job is in a different country. Write a list of advantages and disadvantages of working far from home.

WHAT MAKES A MUSLIM COMMUNITY DIFFERENT FROM OTHERS?

STUDENT NARRATOR: It was Amele's turn to catch question fever now. She wanted to know if Islam is the same everywhere in the world. Her parents said that in her country, which is called Bosnia now, many Muslims had been afraid to show their religion. They were forced into a war when their country—called Yugoslavia—broke up. Amele asked if Muslims in other countries have problems. We learned about problems in many Muslim communities.

Abla Amina: Amele is asking some important questions. We have been looking at the land, the resources and the workers in Muslim regions. We still don't know much about how people live as Muslims in those places. How can we tell that a community is Muslim? What makes Muslim communities different from other communities?

Nabil: Every Muslim community has masajid. We saw some information about building new ones and fixing old ones in Central Asia.

Anas: I saw so many masajid in Egypt. You can hear the *adhan* all over the cities and villages.

Abla Amina: Good thinking! What else shows you how Muslim communities are different? Who else knows where to find information?

Nada: Most people in Muslim countries dress in Islamic ways. There are many different kinds of dress for men and women.

Khadija: Muslims use Islamic sayings. My friend's mother is from Pakistan. I don't understand her when she talks, but I hear her saying *"al-hamdu lillah,"* and *"as-salaamu 'alaikum"* and *"in sha' Allah."* Arabic words are mixed in with Urdu, the language most Pakistanis speak.

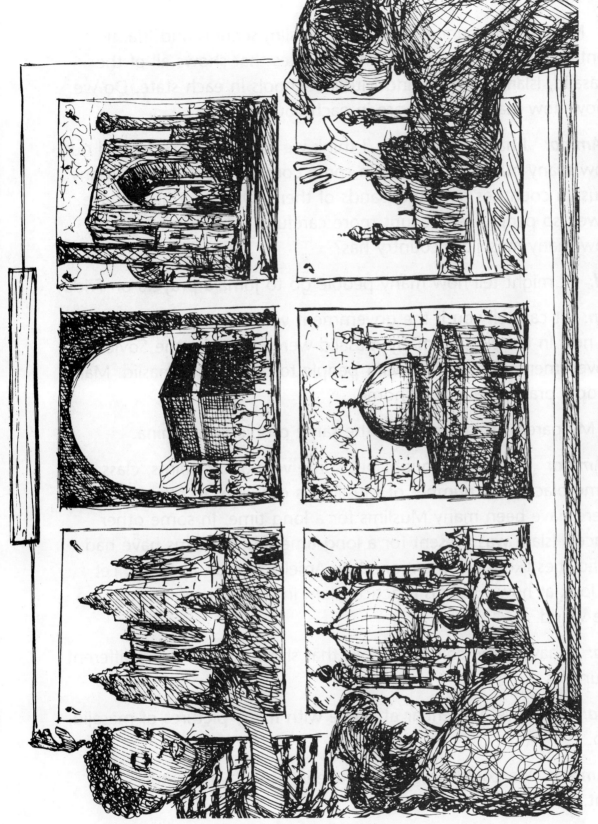

Rahma, Nur, and Zaid are tacking their drawings of masajid to the bulletin board for display. These masajid are in several different countries and cities. Can you identify the famous masajid? They are: 1. the Ka'aba, Makkah; 2. the Dome of the Rock, Jerusalem; 3. Jamia Masjid, Kuala Lumpur, Malaysia; 4. a tiled masjid in Samarkand, Uzbekistan; 5. a masjid in Shenzhen, China; 6. a beautiful mud-brick masjid in Timbuktu, Mali. Which is which?

Abla Amina: Yes, Khadija. Many languages have adopted Arabic words because of Islam.

Zaid: Muslim communities also have Muslim schools and Islamic centers. I saw a map of the United States that shows all of the masajid, Islamic centers and Muslim schools in each state. Do we know how many masajid are in each country?

Abla Amina: I have seen it, too. I think we might be able to find out how many masajid there are in some countries, but not all. Many Muslim countries have thousands of them. Other countries have fewer, so people keep count more carefully. Why is it important how many masajid a country has?

Sayyid: It might tell how many people go to Juma'a prayers on Friday.

Burhan: It can tell you if the government wants people to be Muslim or not. In Uzbekistan, many masajid were closed by the Soviet government. They didn't want people to pray in the masjid. Many people prayed secretly at home.

Nur: My parents told me about the same problems in China.

Abla Amina: You have brought out some very good points, class. In some places, the number of Muslims is growing. In other places, there have been many Muslims for a long time. In some other places, Islam was present for a long time, but Muslims have had difficulties like those mentioned by Amele, Burhan and Nur. Let us look at how Muslims practice Islam in different regions around the world.

Fatima: I have some coloring books that show masajid from different countries.

Khadija: We have a calendar at home with many pictures of masajid, too.

Abla Amina: We could decorate a bulletin board with pictures like that.

Muhammad: I have a poster of the Ka'aba. Omar made a model Ka'aba last year. We could bring them to class, too.

Learning About Islam in the Community

Abla Amina: Your display is beautiful! The pictures show that masajid can have many different shapes and colors. They can be large and small, plain or fancy. They are built of so many different materials! You have shown us quite a few, but there are surely many, many more.

Amele: Is everything about Islam around the world as different as masajid??

Anas: I don't think so. Everyone prays the same way in a masjid, no matter what it looks like.

Abla Amina: That's right. What other activities are important to a Muslim community? What are things that everyone does the same way?

Ali: Muslims everywhere celebrate Islamic 'id. They don't celebrate holidays like Christmas. Muslims everywhere fast in Ramadan. People who aren't Muslim eat in the daytime when we are fasting. In Muslim communities, all of the people celebrate together. Here, you only feel that it's 'id when you go to the masjid.

Sayyid: Muslims everywhere also learn the Qur'an. They all say it in Arabic. Like me, even though I speak Urdu and English, I still have to learn to read the Qur'an in Arabic.

Abla Amina: Good! Learning about Islam is a very important part of a Muslim community. We must learn to recite Qur'an, and we must also learn to understand it. There are many other branches of Islamic knowledge, too. What are some of them?

Omar: Sunna—we learn about Prophet Muhammad's life, and about his sayings, the Hadith.

Nada: We study what Muslims have to do every day, and what laws we are supposed to follow.

Abla Amina: That is called *fiqh*. It means understanding. It is one of the Islamic sciences. Knowledge about Islamic law takes many years to learn. Muslim communities need schools and colleges in all of the Muslim regions we studied. Schools have been important in helping the community to keep Islam strong. What workers does a school need?

Muhammad: They need teachers and students. Our teachers are from many countries. Is that how all Muslim countries are?

Abla Amina: In the U.S., Muslims from many places live in communities together. Muslim teachers that know Arabic and Islamic knowledge often travel to help teach Muslim students in other countries. Malaysia and Indonesia send students to study Islam in Cairo, Makkah and Baghdad, for example. Arabic teachers travel from the Middle East to Africa, Asia and America to teach their language and Islamic knowledge. What are some other ways to learn about Islam?

Khadija: We can get books from libraries and book stores. We can read magazines and newspapers. I have lots of stories and magazines for Muslims at home. We can use Islamic computer programs.

Abla Amina: Excellent! Are all of your books in Arabic?

Khadija: No, I have some in English, too.

Nabil: I have some books in Urdu.

Nur: My mom gets some magazines in Chinese. I still have trouble reading them, though.

Nada: We have Turkish books and some cassettes.

Ali: In Kenya, children learn Ki-swahili. I even saw some books about Swahili in our library. I know a book about the alphabet with words in Swahili.

Abla Amina: Muslims around the world use many languages to learn and write about Islam. But we all try to learn Arabic, and we must use it for prayers and reciting Qur'an. In each community, it is important to have many who know Arabic. However, to help everyone understand what the religion says, Muslims use many other languages. Persian and Turkish, Urdu and Swahili, and languages of Asia are used for many Islamic books, magazines and newspapers. Many other languages are used, too, like French, English, Spanish, Chinese and other Asian and African languages.

Living in Peace or Not?

Amele: My parents said that in Bosnia, Muslims were not allowed to have their own schools when they were young. My father said he is sad, because he wants to learn more about Islam. When I visited the masjid in Bosnia before we left, there were not very many people praying there. Many of them were older people, like my grandfather. Here, the masjid is always full on Friday.

Abla Amina: Amele is bringing an important new idea for our study of Muslims in the world. We started our study by looking at the map that shows where Muslims live. What did the different colors mean?

Muhammad: They showed which countries have mostly Muslim populations. They showed other countries that have many Muslims, or half, or fewer.

Abla Amina: In many places where most of the people are Muslim, they have many masajid and Islamic schools. People speak and write about Islam in books, magazines and newspapers. Muslims learn and try to practice Islam in their lives.

Zaid: We try to do that here, in our school, don't we? In this country, most of the people are not Muslims.

Abla Amina: There are laws and rights here that allow people to practice their religion. Not all governments have such laws. In some areas where most of the people are Muslim, Islam was even forbidden. The parents of Burhan and Nur, from Uzbekistan and

The students made posters about problems in Muslim countries. Amele points to a picture of some of her relatives. Her family was not certain of their safety because of the war. Omar is pinning up a map of Palestine, showing the West Bank and Gaza Strip. The Palestinian flag is displayed on the table. Nabil shows pictures from magazines about the war in Afghanistan. He shows a carpet with a design of helicopters and fighter planes. The Afghani people suffered bombing and loss of their homes and families. Sayyid did a project about Kashmir.

China, experienced those problems. They spoke about the government closing masajid. Amele told us about that problem in Bosnia. Those governments did not believe that people should care about religion at all! They tried to force people to think as officials in the government did. Could you prepare reports about these problems? We should learn about places where Muslims are suffering.

[Later . . .]

STUDENT NARRATOR: Amele, Nabil and Omar collected maps and pictures about the difficulties in their countries. Nur and Burhan reported how people prayed and tried to learn about Islam even though the government tried to stop them. Muslim teachers were sent to prison and even killed. There were only a few masajid and schools left in the country. In government schools, the teachers told students that religion is bad. Someone who showed belief in Islam might lose his job and go hungry. Muslims were not allowed to visit Makkah for hajj.

Omar: In Palestine, we have problems, too. Our country has been occupied for a long time by the Israeli army. People have a hard time, not just about Islam, but in everything in their lives. They have a hard time getting work. The Israelis have often closed schools and shops and kept people in their houses. Many Palestinians were forced to leave the country. There has been a lot of fighting for a long time. People are sad and angry. We hope these problems will end soon.

Amele: The place on the map called Bosnia used to be part of Yugoslavia. Then the country broke up, and people began to fight over how much land would be in each new part. Some of my family is still in Bosnia. We hope they are still all right. We hope that our country will survive. Soldiers from many countries have come. They say that they tried to help, but they did not stop the Serbian army from destroying and killing and taking land. The war is terrible. Many families lost their homes. Many people have died.

Nabil: In Afghanistan, we had to fight against the Russian soldiers for many years. They wanted to take over Afghanistan. The soldiers destroyed many cities and villages. They dropped bombs from the sky that hurt many people. Many families fled the country. That's how my parents came here, to get us away from the fighting.

Sayyid: Pakistan, Kashmir and Bangladesh are three Muslim countries. They used to be part of India. India says that Kashmir belongs to it, but most Kashmiris disagree. People there have a lot of trouble with the Indian government. Many people have died or gone to prisons.

Abla Amina: There are many other places where Muslims have great difficulties. We should remember them in our *du'a* every day. We Muslims who are fortunate to live in peace should try to help others. What can Muslims do to help each other?

Helping Around the World

Khadija: My father travels to other countries for meetings. He says that Muslim writers and scientists talk about their books and other projects. He flies to Malaysia, to Africa and to London sometimes.

Omar: My father is a doctor. He has a clinic. He goes there after work at the hospital. Poor people come to him when they get sick and can't pay.

Fatima: When the earthquake happened in Egypt, my mother and sisters helped collect money, medicine and clothes to help the people there.

Abla Amina: Earthquakes happen in many Muslim regions from Egypt to Turkey, Iran and Central Asia. Floods and storms are another kind of disaster that occurs in some places, like Bangladesh. Lack of rain is another problem. Without rain, crops cannot grow, so people go hungry.

Nada: My sister helps with computer work in an office downtown. They collect money to help poor people. My sister said she saw many pictures of hungry children that made her cry. She wishes that more people would help.

Anas: My mother is a teacher. She also writes books and stories to teach children about Islam and Muslims.

Khadija: We can also help collect food and clothing, and help raise money to help people who are sick or poor, or who have lost their homes.

Abla Amina: These are all important ways for Muslims to help others. Muslims should give time, money and effort to help the community. That is called charity. It is an important Islamic duty. Without charity, the community will not grow, or even survive. Governments and individuals that have wealth should share it with less fortunate people.

Thinking About Section 7:

1. Draw a picture or write about a masjid you might build. What would it look like? Where would you like to build it? What resources will you use in the building?

2. Write a diary of a Muslim for one day. Mention all of the things that Muslims everywhere do in the same way <u>each day</u>. What things do all Muslims do <u>each year</u> in the same way?

3. What languages are spoken in your home? Are they different from the ones you speak at school? What alphabets do you use?

4. Make a list of important things that each Muslim community needs to do. Beside each item, suggest how children can help to do them.

5. Learn more about a country where Muslims are suffering hardship. Collect newspaper and magazine clippings. Ask your parents to help find television programs about it. Ask your teacher or librarian to help you find books and other sources. Make a report to the class.

OUR HERITAGE FAIR— A SCHOOL PARTY

STUDENT NARRATOR: The last part of our study was the most fun. By this time, our exhibits had already filled the classroom and the hall. Now, we were about to take over the whole school! We had a big party in the cafeteria and a show in the auditorium. We invited the rest of the school, our parents and neighbors of the school. This is how it began.

Abla Amina: You have done some wonderful work. We have learned about the lands, resources, the work, lives and communities of Muslims all over the world. We talked about some of their problems. We have seen how Muslims practice Islam in much the same way, no matter where they live or what language they speak. What else would you like to learn about?

Zaid: I guess I started this whole thing, but I still have one more question. Muslims live in many different places. Those places do not always have the same geography or resources, or governments or languages. Islam is Islam no matter where you go. When I visit my friends' houses, they all look about the same. Do they live in the same way everywhere?

Anas: Not in Egypt, that's for sure. Our house here looks so different from there. The trees, the way people look, and what they eat are different, too. I had to get used to it, at first.

Sayyid: That's true for me, too. Here, my family lives in an apartment. When we go to visit my grandparents, aunts and uncles, they live in big houses with a lot of families together. We have so much fun playing with our cousins.

Rahma: It's that way in Senegal, too. We went to visit a village where my mother's uncle lives. The houses looked so different from the ones in the city. Many women cooked together and a lot of families ate together.

Ibrahim: When I first came here, I really missed our house in Indonesia. We used to have a pet monkey in the back yard. It was always warm enough to play outside. We never wore heavy jackets there.

Different Foods and Dress

Abla Amina: Before we finish our study of Muslims around the world, we should find out about the things that make us different, just like kinds of ice cream. Each one is sweet, but they come in different flavors and colors. What are some of those differences?

Khadija: People from different countries wear different kinds of clothes. Some like bright colors, some wear black or white. We could have a parade and a show if everyone wore the dress from their country!

Fatima: Great idea! We could invite the other classes, and even our parents. We could put together all of our projects in a big exhibit.

Zaid: We could have a party with different kinds of food, too.

Abla Amina: Each family could bring a dish from their country and tell its name and what is in it. I'm sure you will find ingredients that show some of the resources and crops we studied earlier. We could even make a recipe book to take home. What else can we have in our show?

Nur: My father loves to tell stories. He said that in China, they have contests to see who can tell the best story. We could have jokes, songs and stories from each country.

Abla Amina: That is a great idea. There are some books in the library with stories, especially folk tales from many lands. You can also collect some from home. To get permission, and more ideas, we can write a note home to your parents. Then we will begin to prepare.

Abla Amina's class posed for a photograph wearing traditional costumes. Rahma is wearing West African dress; Burhan is dressed in turban and kaftan. Nabil wears a fur cap and wide pants. Omar and Muhammad wear different kinds of Arab dress. Zaid decided to wear Moroccan dress, even though he is from the United States. He is standing on the top step. The students had a fine parade.

[Next day . . .]

STUDENT NARRATOR: All of the parents wanted to help. The party would be all day, on a Saturday the following month. We decided to have a bazaar. Some of the students and parents made crafts to sell. The money would go to help the school. I guess our question fever turned into something big! We spent all week getting the exhibits ready.

The Craft Bazaar

Zaid: My father made some wall plaques from wood. They show **calligraphy** designs with Arabic words.

Abla Amina: Those are very nice. **Calligraphy,** designs made from Arabic script, is an art found all over the Muslim world. Verses from Qur'an, sayings of Prophet Muhammad ﷺ, and *du'a*, or prayers, are found in many Muslim homes. Zaid brought one in the shape of a boat.

Omar: My mother brought some embroidery from Palestine. The designs are stitched on cloth. Some are pillows. Some are pictures for the wall. In Palestine, women have dresses covered in these designs. Each stitch is a tiny "X." When you put the different-colored stitches together, they make a design.

Burhan: We brought in some Uzbek hats. Nur has some, too. We can show you how to make them from paper or felt. In our countries, they are made from wool, cotton or silk. They sew fancy designs on the outside. In some places, both men and women wear them. In Uzbekistan, almost all men and boys wear them. My mom gave us some colored silks. She used to work in a factory that makes them. Many women in Central Asia like these bright colors.

Omar: I brought in some fancy trays and vases. They are made of brass. In Syria, Iran and Iraq, many markets sell these things. You can hear the shop before you see it. They hammer the metal—bang! bang! bang!

Sayyid: My father brought some wooden designs. There are trays and boxes. He likes to make them as a hobby. He uses a small chisel to cut little chips out of the wood to make the design. Sometimes he puts in small pieces of pearl.

Nada: Turkey is famous for ceramics like these. Red, blue, white and green. First they make the vase, dish or tile from white clay. Then they paint on the designs, especially flowers and curvy lines. Then they put it in a very hot fire. The design comes out smooth and hard like glass.

Abla Amina: I am sure we will sell many of these things to raise money for the school. These are beautiful examples of Muslim arts and crafts. I'm sure the parents will bring in many more on the day of the exhibit, in sha' Allah.

The Talent Show

STUDENT NARRATOR: For the show, we looked up stories in the library. Burhan found a picture from Uzbekistan. It showed a man named Nasr ad-Din Hoja trying to teach a donkey to read the Qur'an. Burhan told us many jokes about Nasr ad-Din Hoja. Here is one of them:

Burhan: *Nasr ad-Din Hoja bought ten donkeys at the market. He wanted to take them to his farm outside the town. He jumped on the back of one to ride it. To make sure he had all of them, he began to count. 1-2-3-4-5-6-7-8-9. Nasr ad-Din jumped down to look for the lost one. He counted again. 1-2-3-4-5-6-7-8-9-10! They were all there! He jumped back up. Just to make sure, he counted again. Only 9 again! He got down and counted. All ten! Nasr ad-Din shrugged his shoulders and decided to walk. "I'd better walk and have all ten, than ride and lose one!"*

Burhan told many jokes about Nasr ad-Din Hoja. You can see this picture in a book about Central Asia. It shows a photo of a statue in an Uzbeki city square. It is based on a story about Nasr ad-Din Hoja trying to teach a donkey to read! We hope you listen to your teacher better than the donkey did to his! Nasr ad-Din Hoja is known in many Muslim countries and languages. He is also called Abu Nuwwas, Juha or Goha.

Abla Amina: Ha-ha-ha! Nasr ad-Din Hoja is really silly! He is a character found all over the Muslim countries. In some places he is called Abu Nuwwas. In other places he is known as Juha, or Goha. He is always a funny, foolish figure who shows how we all sometimes act foolish.

STUDENT NARRATOR: Then, Nur told a story for the show.

Nur: This story is about Central Asian people who live in round felt houses. They keep animals and move with them by folding up their houses. They have to work hard to have food to eat. Here is the story:

How Lazy Subsutai Was Taught to Work

Once a woman named Bolgun lived in a small village with her son. His name was Subsutai. He was a very lazy son. All day he lay in bed, eating flatbread and poking around in the ashes, or just sleeping.

His mother had no one to help her. She would clean the tent, make the fire, milk the goat. She cooked their meals and did everything else that had to be done. Her back ached, her arms and legs ached from all her work.

No matter how much she asked Subsutai to help, he never did. Finally, she thought of a way to make him work.

One morning, she got up before dawn and tiptoed out of the tent. She set a pot of butter near the door and went back to bed. Then she began to moan. Subsutai woke up, stretched, and said lazily,

"Why are you moaning like that, Mother? You woke me up."

"I don't feel well, son."

"Hey, I'm hungry," he said, "But I can't do any work."

"Don't work," she said, "just look outside and see the weather. Is it cold? I don't want to get worse than I am."

Subsutai thought. "What if my mother really got sick? I would go hungry!" So he put on his coat and went outside. There was a pot of butter! "What luck!" He took three steps out of the tent, three steps back, and the pot was in the tent.

"Look what I found, Mother! Make a pot of tea!"

"Imagine," she said, "first time out, and you found food!"

He was very happy, but then got lazy again and slept the rest of the day.

Next morning, Bolgun put a big piece of meat ten steps from the tent. When Subsutai looked, he felt lucky again. "Just over there was a big piece of mutton!" He took ten steps there, and ten back. "Look at this, Mother. Hurry and cook it!"

They both enjoyed it very much. Subsutai puffed out his chest, "Look what a fine fellow I am! I bring home food. That means I work!"

Well, that is what his mother was waiting to hear. She put the food farther and farther away. Soon, he was going a hundred steps and found a pile of pancakes!

After some time, his mother said, "You're such a lucky person. Why don't you try your luck at hunting? You'll be luckier than any of the neighbors."

So Subsutai put on his quilted jacket, saddled his horse, and off he went. He rode along the steppe, and soon he saw a rabbit. He shot an arrow and missed, and another, and another. He used up all his arrows, got angry and ran after the rabbit. He felt he was a fine worker, and couldn't go home empty-handed. But the rabbit was fast, and ran up and down hills. It leaped over a hole, and Subsutai leaped after it. He couldn't catch it, but Subsutai didn't look like a lazy fellow any more. He was ready to run, but the rabbit was gone.

Subsutai gave up. He looked for his horse, but it was gone, too. He sat on a rock, feeling miserable. He was too hungry and tired even to make it home. As he sat there, he saw something in the grass. He picked it up. It was a golden arrow! No sooner had he tucked it into his jacket, than he saw some men riding toward him. It was the local prince and his men.

"Hey, hunter, have you seen the prince's golden arrow?"

"No," said Subsutai, "But I'm a lucky fellow and I can find it for you. But first, bring me some food and a horse."

As soon as they galloped off, he tossed the arrow under a bush and waited for them. They soon came, and brought him a fine meal. One of the men came leading Subsutai's own horse which he had found.

Subsutai finished eating and wiped his mouth. "Go over to that bush. You'll find the arrow under it."

Sure enough, the men found it. They were amazed at his luck. They thanked him, and the prince gave him many fine gifts. Subsutai returned home with his arms full and showed his mother.

Ever since then, he would saddle his horse at dawn and go off to the hills. They had plenty of meat and warm furs for the winter. Subsutai returned from the hunt and helped his mother with the chores.
He was lazy no more, and happiness had come to their tent.

Abla Amina: Thank you. You told a fine story, Nur. That is a folk tale from the Asian steppe people. They are very good at storytelling. So are you.

Ibrahim: In Indonesia, there are shadow puppet shows. This is how the puppets look. There are monsters, good and bad people. The puppeteers work behind a sheet with a strong light. Drums and bells make sounds in the scary and exciting parts, like thunder and sword fights. I love to watch them! We will show you how they look behind a curtain. They move with sticks.

Abla Amina: Language and the music, stories, poems and songs that different groups enjoy vary among Muslim regions. Here, we have shared some of those things.

Another thing that makes us different is history. **History** is the many different things that happened to people over time. Each place has its own history. How and when Islam first came to a place is an important part of that. Whether the people lived in peace, or whether they often suffered from war is also important. Some countries were ruled by other groups for a long period of time. This changed their schools, their cities and often their way of life.

As we have seen, the land, climate and resources make a big difference in the way people live and work. Language and arts are important in expressing feelings and ideas. All of these things together make up a people's **culture**, or way of life. Islam is an important part of our culture, because beliefs shape our everyday lives. Islam shapes our families and communities, our governments

Our Heritage Fair was a great success! We filled the school with our displays. We had delicious foods from many different places. We showed our parents, teachers and neighbors how much we had learned, and everyone had fun at the talent show. We hope you will try it!

and our history over a long time. Muslim cultures are many, but they have much in common.

Our Party—A Happy Ending

STUDENT NARRATOR: On the Saturday of our big party, everything went as planned. Many people came to visit the school. Even the mayor of the city came, and many people who live in the neighborhood near our school. Abla Amina gave a very nice speech to everyone. We wore special hats and name tags, and gave tours around the exhibits. We had so much food, with balloons and decorations everywhere. The show and the parade were fun, even though some of us got a little nervous. We did fine, though.

Just imagine how one little question could start such a big thing! Some of the work was difficult. We did study very hard, but we all learned some answers to some very new questions. We learned many things about Muslims all around the world. The best part was the party that ended the whole project.

I have told you all of this, and introduced you to our class and our teacher, Abla Amina, so that you can try it. With a little question fever and a lot of work, you could do this in your school. I hope you enjoy the experience as much as we did.

Thinking About Section 8:

1. Pick your family's favorite recipe, or a favorite processed food. Make a list of the ingredients in it. Find out where these products are grown.

2. Find out about the traditional dress of a country not mentioned here. Draw a picture or dress a figure for display.

3. Find a joke, a poem or a story to tell to the group. Name the country where it was first recited, and tell whether it is very old or more modern.

4. List some famous crafts from Muslim countries. Bring some examples from home with your parents' permission. Do a report or project on how these crafts are made (examples: leather work, knotting rugs, dyeing cloth, pottery, knitting, embroidery, calligraphy, metalwork, jewelry).

LIST OF CHARACTERS APPEARING IN EACH SECTION

Section 1
Student Narrator
Abla Amina
Zaid
Muhammad
Fatima
Amele
Nada
Rahma
Omar
Nabil
Nur
Khadija

Section 2
Student Narrator
Abla Amina
Omar
Fatima
Khadija
Muhammad
Anas
Zaid
Nur

Section 3
Student Narrator
Abla Amina
Fatima
Muhammad
Omar
Anas
Rahma
Khadija
Nabil
Zaid
Nur
Ali
Nada
Burhan
Sayyid

Ibrahim
Amele

Section 4
Abla Amina
Zaid
Khadija
Amele
Nur
Muhammad
Omar
Nabil
Fatima
Student Narrator
Rahma
Sayyid
Burhan
Ali
Anas
Nada
Ibrahim

Section 5
Abla Amina
Rahma
Muhammad
Nur
Sayyid
Ibrahim
Omar
Fatima
Burhan
Anas
Nada
Khadija

Section 6
Student Narrator
Abla Amina
Zaid
Khadija

Nabil
Nada
Ibrahim
Fatima
Anas
Nur
Muhammad
Sayyid

Section 7
Student Narrator
Abla Amina
Nabil
Anas
Nada
Khadija
Zaid
Sayyid
Burhan
Nur
Fatima
Muhammad
Amele
Ali
Omar

Section 8
Student Narrator
Abla Amina
Zaid
Anas
Sayyid
Rahma
Ibrahim
Khadija
Fatima
Nur
Omar
Burhan
Nada

Part III

Teaching Suggestions and Enrichment Activities

SECTION 1: MEET THE CLASS

PRE-READING:

1. Flip through the pages of the student text. Ask students to notice some unusual things about the book [written like a play; all the pictures show students].

2. Discuss the title. What is the main idea? Think of different ways to divide lands and people of the world into groups in order to study them.

COMPREHENSION:

3. What is a Muslim school? How is it different from a public school? Do other religious groups have their own schools? Why?

4. How do questions help us to learn? How can students work together to learn about a big subject? Where can we look for information on the subject of this book?

LEARNING NEW CONCEPTS:

5. Think about the word GEOGRAPHY. What places have you already studied? What do we learn about a place from studying geography?

6. Review **climate** and **resources** or introduce and define if unfamiliar to students.

7. DEMONSTRATING PROPORTION WITH COLORED BEANS (math crossover): Repeat the demonstration that Abla Amina does for the class on page 18. Illustrate the proportion of Muslims in the total world population by using quantities of two different colored beads, beans or candies. Take one double handful or large cup measure and place in a heap on the table. Repeat until five equal heaps are displayed in a row. State that this "represents," or stands for, the total world population, "all of the people in the world." Measure out a quantity of contrasting color equal to one of the heaps. Tell the students that this quantity is approximately equal to the number of Muslims in the world population. To show a proportion of the total, tell the students that you will replace one of the five original heaps with the contrasting one. This will show how many of the world's people are Muslim. The teacher may reinforce and manipulate the concept by varying the proportion of each kind. For example, you may demonstrate the proportion of male vs. female, which is roughly 50:50, or use a criterion derived from the students in the class.

ACQUIRING SKILLS:

8. Review the names of the continents and have students point to them on a map or play the identification and puzzle game. Make transparencies or colored, enlarged cutouts of the continents on Worksheets #1a–c. Practice shape and name identification by holding up each cut-out in various sequences and at various speeds. When they have mastered this, have each student make a world map, as follows:

9. MAPPING FROM MEMORY: Use Worksheets #1a–c to make a map from memory. Color and cut out each of the continent outlines. Using a sheet of blue or white 11" x 17"

paper (or other large paper from a roll), fold it in half lengthwise and draw a line in the fold for the equator. Have students arrange the continents on the map from memory. Then have them check their placement with a world map. Check each student's map for correct placement, then have them glue down the continents and decorate their maps with ships, compass rose, borders, etc.

10. Look at some books about Islam and Muslims in the library, and your textbook. Talk about the pictures used. What do these pictures show about the author's ideas about Islam and Muslims?

ENRICHMENT:

11. Take a poll of your class to find out which countries students' families come from. Write the results on a chart. If there are several students from one country, you can make a bar graph to show which country has the most students in the class population. This could be done with the total school population with help from the central office.

12. Plan to visit a Muslim or other private school to discuss the school with a class like yours. What other topics would be interesting to discuss with the students?

SECTION 2: MAPS, COLORS AND BIG NUMBERS

PRE-READING:

1. Review the terms **key, population, census**.

COMPREHENSION:

2. Refer to the poster map *The Muslim World* (Islamic Foundation, Leicester, England, 1994) in the binder pocket as the class reads the section. The map included defines a Muslim country as one where a **majority** (over 50%) of the population is Muslim. Have students locate the map key and read the percentage range for each color used. Practice identifying countries by color used and by percentage.

   For an excellent study of Muslim minorities with regard to numbers, history, living conditions, level of organization attained, and prospects, see Ali Kettani, *Muslim Minorities in the World Today* (Mansell, 1986). Though exact population figures are no longer accurate, his projections have proven durable, and the book remains a unique and valuable study that has not been superseded.

LEARNING NEW CONCEPTS:

3. Discuss the large numbers "million" and "billion." Write them as words and numbers on the board. Count the zeros to find out how many millions it takes to make a billion. A good book on understanding big numbers is David M. Schwartz, *How Much Is a Million?*, illustrated by Steven Kellog (Scholastic Inc, 1985).

4. Define the terms **majority** and **minority** using the map, key and Worksheet #2.

ACQUIRING SKILLS:

5. PERCENTAGE AND PROPORTION: Review or introduce the concept of **percent** as <u>telling how many out of one hundred</u>. Build upon the demonstration of proportion (beans demonstration) by asking what fraction of the world population is Muslim. Convert this to a percentage, or fraction whose denominator is 100. Thus, 20 out of 100 people in

the world are Muslim, or 20%. Another common way of expressing the proportion is "how many out of ten." Practice working with percentages to make comparisons, using familiar objects in the room. Possibilities include the number of students having a certain color of clothing or book bag, types of shoes, kinds of food in their lunches. Think of other useful ideas for using percentages to compare things, like the amount of time spent in school, sleeping, eating, doing homework, playing and watching TV.

6. PERCENTAGE VS. ABSOLUTE NUMBER (math crossover): Use Worksheet #2 to accompany the discussion on page 23 about small countries with large percentages vs. large countries with small percentages. The object of the lesson is to explain graphically that small percentages of population can, in a large country, amount to substantial numbers of people.

ENRICHMENT:

7. An interesting demographic map in the *Rand McNally Picture Atlas of the World* (Brian Delf, 1991), entitled "Where People Live" (p. 12), shows pictographs of people stacked to compare the population of each continent. Asia has by far the largest. Statistically, the demographic center of the Muslim world is said to be Lahore, Pakistan, there being an equal number of Muslims living to the east as to the west of that city.

8. Look up information about how governments collect and process census data using computers today.

9. Look up the population of selected countries in the atlas or other sources. Do the calculator activity in the section questions, #5, using the percentage range and population figures to arrive at the lowest and highest numbers for Muslim population.

SECTION 3: PLACES WHERE MANY MUSLIMS LIVE

NOTE: It is essential that the students follow along on a map as they read the students' reports in the student text dialogue. A classroom wall map, individual classroom atlases, or small-group sessions with a large reference atlas are good possibilities.

Acquire a PHYSICAL MAP, which is the closest type of map to what you would see if you took a photo from outer space. The advantage of a physical relief map is that it gives an indication of desert, forest, grassland and tundra that helps students to visualize the relationship between topography, climate and the kinds of human activity that are possible. These maps can be compared to climate and vegetation maps. An excellent set of physical relief maps is in the *National Geographic Atlas of the World*, and some classroom wall maps and laminated desk maps are also of this type. Elevation maps are probably the least useful, since the earth tone colors used often cause confusion in students, who imagine that the colors represent the situation on the ground.

Comprehension may be enhanced by using laminated desk maps with erasable markers. Students may be asked to outline each region under discussion, to identify topographical features mentioned in the text, and the teacher can check for comprehension. The teacher may build upon the text by discussing additional features not mentioned in the text.

PRE-READING:

1. Introduce.or review various types of maps. Show examples of elevation maps, climate maps, resource maps, population maps. Show some satellite images of parts of the globe. Tell how to use the key to distinguish among them and discuss what each is used for.

COMPREHENSION / LEARNING NEW CONCEPTS:

2. Define the word *ummah* and write it in Arabic, using Worksheet #3. Discuss several Qur'an verses on the topic of the Muslim *ummah*, its meaning and application. Discuss the concept of local, regional, national and international levels of Muslim community. Use the Qur'an verses to illuminate the meaning of the *ummah* to all Muslims, and our responsibilities to it.

3. Discuss the term **region** as a way of dividing up large areas of land and water so that we can study it more easily. Explain that these divisions are convenient, but artificial. Ask the students to consider a world map and give ideas for logical divisions. They might mention ideas like division into hemispheres and continents.

4. Follow each section of the text, having some students read the parts of the students in the play aloud while others point to the features they describe on a physical relief wall map, if possible, or laminated maps, as discussed.

5. Define **landforms** as the shape and features of the land. Check for comprehension of vocabulary words in the text, such as **desert, grasslands (savanna and steppe), plateau, peninsula, mountain chain, sea, coast, river valley, tropical**.

6. Define and explain **majority** and **minority**, using the map key, and build upon the activities in Section 1, #7 and Section 2, #6. Use examples from students in the classroom (hair color, shoe style, male/female), or use different colored objects in a jar like beads or beans (See Section 1, #5). Transfer the concept to populations, and finally apply to Muslims in the total population of a given country. Locate countries on the map where Muslims form the majority and minorities of various sizes.

ACQUIRING SKILLS:

7. MAP CONCENTRATION GAME: To reinforce the information given in this lesson, a kind of "Concentration" can later be played in small groups. Practice locating physical features like rivers, mountain ranges, deserts and bodies of water. Then study the map carefully. Using the eastern hemisphere of a large physical map as a base, cover each continent with numbered 3"–4" (10 cm) squares of cardboard. Use the list of "Places to Remember" at the end of the student text, and have the students add to it. Then, one student or the teacher calls out the name of a geographic feature, and the student must lift the correct cardboard square. First try gets 10 points, second try 5 points, third 1 point. After three tries, another student gets to try. The one with the highest score after 10 rounds wins.

ENRICHMENT:

8. It is a good idea to purchase a large, physical relief poster map for this unit, and to make transparency overlays, icons, and labels showing the areas studied. The project can begin with this unit by marking out the boundaries of Muslim majority countries and Muslim regions within large countries like China and the former Soviet Union. This

ongoing class project will save the time required to prepare individual maps, or supplement the effort. Most important, it will help the students to connect information from the various sections of the text, and to reinforce the relationship between place, location and human use of the environment.

9. Write a poem using Worksheet #3, draw pictures or make posters illustrating the meaning of the Muslim *ummah* and the ways Muslims connect with and cooperate with one another locally, regionally and on a global basis. Posters might also illustrate the concept of diversity and unity.

SECTION 4: USING RESOURCES IN PLACES WHERE MUSLIMS LIVE

PRE-READING / COMPREHENSION:

1. Review **resource**. Have students brainstorm a list of resources. On the chalkboard, make categories for the resources listed (plants, minerals, animals, fuels, land, water, etc.).

LEARNING NEW CONCEPTS:

2. Define **urban** and **rural**. Discuss the meaning of the chart of urban/rural population proportion in the text, page 50. Ask students why this information is considered important to know about a country. Use an atlas or a gazetteer like the *Dorling Kindersley World Reference Atlas* (see bibliography) to study the proportion of urban and rural population in various countries. Encourage students to make generalizations and look for patterns regarding this information.

3. FARMING, IRRIGATION AND WATER USE: These three related topics are merely sketched out in the text. The topic of agricultural products is introduced from the beginning in relation to availability of water. Draw attention to the fact that apart from a few crops and agricultural products that can be grown in fairly dry conditions (livestock grazing [camels, goats, sheep, cattle and horses], date palms [on oases], olives, incense), most require irrigation if rainfall is insufficient (fruits and vegetables, grains, peanuts, beans and cotton). Some require a great deal of rainfall, usually in a tropical wet or moist mountain climate (bananas, pineapple, sugar cane, tea and coffee, spices, rubber, rice).

Define **irrigation**. Discuss the two ways of watering crops (rainfall and irrigation). Illustrate the various means of irrigating crops shown and discussed in the text, asking students what conditions are required for each (presence of a river, presence of underground water supplies, presence of mountain snow runoff). In discussing the various types of irrigation pictured and mentioned in the text, ask students which ones need the most organization and the most workers to complete (building canals from a river, building and maintaining qanat, building dams, building desalinization plants).

4. Define **industry**. The discussion of industries contains a number of concepts that may be new to some students. They include **textiles, petroleum, natural gas, processing, consumer, export goods**. The questions within the text and at the end of Section 4 help to define and clarify these concepts. Have the students give examples of each item.

ACQUIRING SKILLS:

5. MAKING MODEL HOUSES: Do the activity described in the text by having the students research homes in various Muslim regions. *Aramco World Magazine* back issues are very useful, as are the country studies listed among the books for student reading in

the bibliography of this unit. Using cardboard bases, mailing tubes, plastic bottles and tin cans, students may build up details using construction paper, fabrics, clay, aluminum foil, wooden craft sticks and natural materials. Alternatively, students may make posters or drawings of the houses for display.

6. ASSESSING ENVIRONMENTAL IMPACT: Make a chart discussing the costs and benefits, and giving examples of each type of water use mentioned. Helpful reading for the teachers is the *National Geographic* article "The Middle East's Water: Critical Resource" (183:5 [May 1993]). Discuss relevant verses from Qur'an about different ways Allah (SWT) supplied water to us. In discussing the environmental impact of water use, it is important to weave into the discussion Islamic values relevant to human custodianship of the earth, the need to take care of finite resources, and avoidance of pollution. A sample chart, like a cost/benefit analysis, is given below. Students may be asked for their views evaluating the results of the analysis.

Type of Water Project	Benefits	Costs	Example
1. dam	water for farming, electric power, controls floods from natural river	big lake floods land, people moved, less water for countries downstream, often disturbs fishing	Aswan Dam, Ataturk Dam
2. canals from river	water for farming, factories, cities	less water flow, sea dries up, salty land	Amu and Syr Darya, Aral Sea disaster
3. sea water desalinization	can build cities and farms in desert, big supply	uses a lot of energy, costs much money, needs pipelines	Kuwait, Saudi Arabia
4. qanats	crops in dry places, uses ready supply	difficult to build and keep up	Iran, North Africa, Western China
5. deep wells	crops in desert, pure water, big, nearby supply	expensive to drill, can't replace supply	all over Middle East

7. UNDERGROUND RESOURCES: Study the chart on page 63 showing the most important minerals and other underground resources in Muslim regions. Draw students' attention to the fact that the most prominent resources in the Muslim lands are petroleum and gas, and that other minerals are not so abundant. However, it is important to note that desert conditions make exploration and extraction difficult, so new resources may yet be discovered. Resources listed in various sources may be only those currently being extracted, or known reserves (encyclopedia entries tend to be more inclusive).

Students may research some other important minerals used today that are NOT found in Muslim regions in order to determine what raw materials Muslim countries must import for their industries. Another important component of the discussion of resources is their environmental impact at the site of extraction, manufacture and post-consumer. Discuss recycling and conservation.

8. INDUSTRY: Define industry. Discuss the relationship between natural resources and industries. Study the chart on page 62 made by Omar and Anas to avoid listing the same industries repeatedly for all the Muslim countries.

   COMPUTER PROJECT: With the assistance of a computer teacher and students, consider alternative ways to set up the database so that the information can be sorted. What criteria might be used to sort? (Countries with the most industries to those with least, the most common industries in Muslim countries, number of countries with a certain industry.) How does sorting data add to our understanding? A similar database chart might be made to list underground resources such as metals, fossil fuels, and other minerals. Students may decide which graphic form of the information—map or chart—is most useful.

9. DEVELOPMENT: Discuss the importance of developing industries in a country, in order to meet the basic needs of the population, to help the economy and to create jobs. The latter subject receives extensive discussion in Section 5.

10. Discuss EXPORT GOODS, particularly those that use the skills of workers rather than the natural resources of a country to make money. Have the children name some products that are made of many parts. (Consider cars, video games, a computer, television or refrigerator.) Tell them that the parts are often manufactured in many different places, and put together, or **assembled** at yet another location. Nowadays, countries that want to increase manufacturing offer advantages to companies that bring in all the parts and have them put together. There are many examples in Muslim countries: North Africa and Southeast Asia manufacture clothing, small appliances; Malaysian workers, especially women, make computer chips and other parts, and put together electronic equipment.

ENRICHMENT:

11. Look at the agricultural and animal products of selected Muslim countries, using a resource map, encyclopedia, or atlas. Make a list of processed foods that might be made in the country's food processing factories. Which countries are likely to have fishing industries? Dairy products? Leather, meat and wool? Preserved fruits? Peanuts and cooking oils? Find recipes in a cookbook that use these products, and prepare some for the class.

SECTION 5: GOOD LOCATION CAN BE A RESOURCE!

PRE-READING:

1. Define **location** and ask students why a good location might be important. Ask in what type of location the students would most like to live. Conversely, what sorts of amenities would they like to have located near their house. (Distinguish between needs and wants.)

2. Review or introduce vocabulary words: **port, service job, tourist, skills**. Introduce the idea that being in a good location helps people to earn a living.

COMPREHENSION / LEARNING NEW CONCEPTS:

3. Discuss the importance of LOCATION relative to geographic features (**landforms**), to resources, to transport and to climate. For example, Antarctica is very rich in resources, but it has no permanent population. Have students use a map to fill in the <u>graphic</u>

<u>organizer</u> in the text page 67, or use Worksheet #8, identifying and locating cities and associating them with geographic features (rivers, coastlines, harbors, etc.). Locate places where many cities are grouped together. Do clusters of cities seem to have anything to do with transportation? Are there rivers, lakes, **coasts** or **harbors** nearby? Why are cities often located near the narrow places between two bodies of water? <u>Discuss how changes in transportation have changed the importance of certain locations</u>. For example, caravan cities mentioned in the text are less important since people no longer use overland transport.

4. TOURISM: Explain that many countries depend upon **tourists**, or visitors from other countries, as a kind of industry. It can bring in millions of dollars each year. Have students list things that tourists might need or want to spend money on (hotels, food, transportation, entertainment, shopping, local arts and crafts, etc.). See enrichment activity #10, this section, below.

ACQUIRING SKILLS / ENRICHMENT:

5. Use *The Muslim World Map* or an atlas to learn the names and location of important cities. The teacher may make a memory game by covering the names of important cities on the map with paper or removable correction tape and asking students to name them from memory. A blank outline map may also be used for this purpose. Accurately place dots for 5–10 (or more) prominent cities in Muslim countries and have a contest to see who can name the most.

6. Use Worksheet #4 as a guide for individual or group research on cities in Muslim regions. Make an info-cube showing the following information on each of the six sides. The cubes, which can be reproduced in any size, will make a nice classroom display or exhibit. Suggested topics for research from the worksheet are as follows:

> 1. Name of city, country, important river or other location
> 2. Population, area, whether it is a capital
> 3. Important jobs or functions of the city
> 4. A short, famous story about the city
> 5. One or more famous buildings or places
> 6. Facts about a famous Muslim from the city

7. Look up TOURIST ATTRACTIONS in your city or state or selected Muslim countries. Make short reports or bulletin board displays. Embassies and travel agencies often have illustrated brochures. Make a chart of reasons people like to visit these countries, and place the examples of tourist attractions in the correct categories: good climate in winter/summer; beaches for swimming, mountains for hiking and skiing; historic buildings and ruins; beautiful scenery; etc.

SECTION 6: PEOPLE ARE THE MOST IMPORTANT RESOURCE FOR A COUNTRY

PRE-READING:

1. Consider the section title by discussing the difference between natural and human resources. List ways in which people are important resources.

COMPREHENSION / LEARNING NEW CONCEPTS:

2. Review the importance of LOCATION in helping people to make a good living, and relate it to earning a living. Use an analogy like two students selling lemonade on a hot day. Which one will make more money, the one next to the busy playground, or the one on a quiet, shady street two blocks away? Review definitions of **service workers** and **producers**.

3. WORKERS, SKILLS AND EDUCATION: Ask students why many people today feel it is so important to go to school. How does education help people earn a living? How do countries help educate citizens (build schools, hire teachers, buy books and equipment, and pass laws that children must go to school). Why is education important to a country's economy? What would happen if a country had no workers who knew how to tell time, read, write, or use numbers?

ACQUIRING SKILLS:

4. Use the dictionary to look up DEVELOPMENT. Make a WORD WEB or SEMANTIC MAP to explain the kinds of activities that people and governments engage in to build the country. Begin with categories like "factories," "transportation," "communication," "education," "trade," "standard of living" and "community and government," then fill in specific examples and details. Some categories may intersect with others. Each class will come up with a different structure and content. The most important element is student participation.

5. WORKERS ON THE MOVE: Use the chart that Abla Amina put on the blackboard to help understand why countries bring in and send out workers. For comprehension, have the students explain what other reasons for travel by workers are mentioned in the text (training, teaching, Islamic work, businessmen travel to get new products and ideas, etc.). In addition to the examples in the text (Saudi Arabia, Algeria, Turkey), the teacher can add to the examples for case #1, the Gulf States, Iraq (before the war); and for #2, Egypt, Tunisia, the Philippines, Pakistan, and numerous other countries whose emigration for economic reasons is high. The teacher can also enhance the necessarily sketchy information in the text by explaining that some Muslims from the #2 countries migrate to non-Muslim countries in Europe (Italy, France, Germany, etc., or in the special case of Israel), while others migrate to Arab countries that are #1 cases. Note that increasingly, the #1 case Arab countries are bringing in laborers from South and Southeast Asia, both Muslim and non-Muslim. It is also worthy of note that Palestinians were among the first group of Muslim workers from a #2 country (occupied by the Israelis and hence lacking development and jobs for Muslims) who became highly educated as a group and fulfilled the need of oil-producing states for skilled labor. Many have also taken jobs and built businesses in the United States, South America and West Africa, as have groups of Lebanese.

ENRICHMENT:

6. Have students bring in LETTERS AND PHOTOS OF RELATIVES and/or acquaintances who are working far from their home countries. Look at the stamps on the letters and the background in photos and try to get clues about the countries. Find out what work they do in the country, why they went there, and how they enjoy their lives there.

7. Bring in one or several GUEST SPEAKERS who could be described as emigrant workers, whether just starting out in a menial job or a professional or professor. Many of the Islamic teachers employed by masajid and other institutions qualify. Have the students prepare questions to ask about why they came, whether they find life easier here or in their home country, what advantages and disadvantages they experience, etc. Students may also CONDUCT INTERVIEWS in lieu of a guest speaker. The class could use a uniform questionnaire for the interviews and then compare the results.

SECTION 7: WHAT MAKES A MUSLIM COMMUNITY DIFFERENT FROM OTHERS?

PRE-READING:

1. Review the sorts of information that the class has gathered so far. Are these things common to every community? (Products, resources, landforms, climate, jobs, cities, etc.)

2. Ask what makes it apparent that a place is inhabited by Muslims (dress, presence of masajid, sound of *athan* and Qur'an in streets, Islamic expressions in the languages, etc.).

COMPREHENSION:

3. FEATURES OF MUSLIM COMMUNITIES: Read aloud the conversation that introduces the section. What points are the students raising with their questions and ideas?

   • How can a Muslim community be distinguished from any other?

   • What features of everyday life do all Muslims share?

   • Is the number of masajid in a place important in telling about the community's life?

   • How does government disapproval of Islam affect the community?

   • Think of some other groups in history who were not allowed to live according to their beliefs and culture.

4. ISLAMIC EDUCATION: Ask students to name educational settings where they have learned about Islam, recited Qur'an and met with other Muslim children. What activities do their parents engage in, either educational or service for the Muslim community? Do they take place close to home or do they sometimes require travel to other states or countries? Why are these activities important? How do they help to build the community? Discuss daily, weekly and annual events in which Muslims from various communities participate. How do local, national and international activities differ? What kinds of people participate in each?

LEARNING NEW CONCEPTS:

5. Discuss the implications of LIVING AS MEMBERS OF A MAJORITY OR A MINORITY. How is a Muslim community affected by its relative numbers? Guide the students to think about the ways communities make decisions about laws, education and important

projects needed by the community. Make a list of examples on how being in the minority can be more difficult.

6. With reference to the above discussion, introduce the concept of TOLERANCE. What does it mean to tolerate others' beliefs, ways of life and values? Which countries mentioned in the text have not seemed tolerant toward Muslim majorities and minorities? (China, the former Soviet Union and Yugoslavia, etc.) What sorts of problems exist for Muslims who must live in a situation of intolerance? How is intolerance communicated to people? (Person-to-person, in schools, on TV and radio, by laws.) How are adults and children affected?

7. Discuss the ATTITUDES MUSLIMS SHOULD DISPLAY, according to the Qur'an and Sunnah towards citizens with other beliefs, and how they should react to intolerance. Why did Prophet Muhammad ﷺ teach tolerance? Does it make a difference in how Muslims treat others whether they are themselves a minority or a majority? Why or why not?

8. CONFLICTS IN MUSLIM REGIONS: Discuss the examples mentioned in the text (Bosnia, Central and South Asia, Palestine). The amount of additional information beyond the brief sketches given by the students will depend upon teachers' judgment of the class' ability and interest. Students may undertake individual or group study on some other flash-points of difficulty or long-standing situations of persecution and intolerance. An interesting grade-level source on the conflict in Lebanon is *A Time of Troubles*, by F. P. Heide and J. H. Gilliand (Clarion Books, 1992). On Palestine, *Sitti and the Cats* (Roberts Reinhard, 1993) and *Sitti's Secrets* (Four Winds Press, 1994) are good stories for this age level. Uthman Hutchinson has written a collection of stories for various grade levels, among which *The Cave* and *Great Grandpa's Story (I and II)* discuss the theme of living through colonialism, war and conflict (Amana Publications, 1995).

ACQUIRING SKILLS:

9. Use the map poster *Muslims in the United States* (American Muslim Council, 1995) to discuss how a minority community builds to meet its needs. Use the map colors and bar graph to see where the largest populations of Muslims in the U.S. are located. Count the number of Islamic centers and schools in various states. The teacher will need to assist the students to understand the graphs included with the map.

USING THE KEY TO ADD INFORMATION TO A MAP (*Muslims in the United States*, American Muslim Council, 1995): In addition to numerous masajid in Michigan, there are twelve (12) schools. These have been left off of the map. Have the students make copies of the symbol for an Islamic school, and paste them on the map. Alternatively, use one symbol, and place a small number "12" above it. The geographic distribution of the schools corresponds approximately to the distribution of masajid.

10. Examine the masajid pictured in the students' drawings and on *The Muslim World Map* Poster. What materials have been used in construction? How do the styles differ from region to region?

11. Use newspapers, interviews with parents and library resources to find out information on places where Muslims are currently experiencing hardship because of war, natural disaster or poverty. Make posters or bulletin board displays using newspaper and magazine clippings and maps. Community leaders can be invited as guest speakers to give information about Muslim charities that help out in these areas. (See follow-up activity on a classroom charity project, #13 this section.)

ENRICHMENT:

12. Examine and color in pages from the *Muslim World Coloring Book*. Take out library books or back issues of *Aramco World Magazine* to find interesting examples of masjid architecture. Another source is *The Book of Mosques*, Luqman Nagy (TaHa Publ., 1993). Students may make short reports on masajid around the world, including a photocopy, postcard or drawing, the country and city where it is found, when it was built (how old it is), and the materials used to build and/or decorate it. This is also a good idea for the info-cube activity as described for Muslim cities in Worksheet #4.

13. MAKE A POSTER ABOUT MUSLIM UNITY OR TOLERANCE IN ISLAM, collecting relevant verses from the Qur'an and Hadith, as well as stories from Islamic history (see stories and other material from IQRA International Education Foundation and the Islamic Foundation) that illustrate examples of these two qualities.

14. DESIGN A CHARITY PROJECT to help in one of the areas identified in #11 this section. This might involve collecting food, clothing or other items for a local community, or it might involve collecting money. If your school is planning a Heritage Day, Community Bazaar, etc., such as the one modeled in Section 7 of this unit, a table for such fund-raising (bake sale, toy sale, display for charity, etc.) could be a part of the activity. Another interesting project that involves no direct transmission of money is to establish contact with Muslim children in one of these areas, sending them letters, drawings or other artwork; copies of the Qur'an; or audio- or videocassette tapes containing stories, songs or personal introductions. Finding out about a school for blind or deaf children, orphans, etc., and establishing contact by such means brings home the reality of children living in other places.

SECTION 8: OUR HERITAGE FAIR—A SCHOOL PARTY

PRE-READING:

1. Explain that the class is about to complete its big project, and in this section, students plan to collect all of their work in a big exhibit for the school. It turns into a party.

2. If your class is following this unit more than passively, the students may wish to put on a similar show and party, inviting other classes, parents, etc. In that case, study of this section would be a good time to gather ideas and begin planning for such an event.

COMPREHENSION:

3. Discuss the points raised in the introductory discussion. What are the differences in ways of life between Muslim countries and non-Muslim, urban and rural in terms of family structure and bonds, types of houses, diet, daily activities, etc. What role does climate play in the differences in our ways of life? How do people's lives change when many family members live nearby or far away?

4. Discuss the differences between village life and city life in Muslim regions. WHAT ACTIVITIES WOULD YOU BE LIKELY TO SEE IF YOU WERE A FLY ON THE WALL IN THOSE PLACES? In order to bring out some of these ideas, you may wish to read *The Day of Ahmed's Secret* (Lothrop, Lee and Shepard, 1990), *Sitti and the Cats* and *Sitti's Secret* (cited above) and other stories about Muslim parts of the world. Perusing *Aramco World Magazine* issues such as those mentioned here also helps to show how others live in rural and urban settings. The books listed in the bibliography under "Books for

Student Reading" also contain many photos and accounts of the way of life in those regions. The *We Live In . . .* series (Bookwright Press) is very well done in this regard, as is the *Then and Now . . .* series (Lerner Publications) on Central Asia. All of the books and articles listed are very useful in giving a picture of life in Muslim regions.

LEARNING NEW CONCEPTS:

5. LITERATURE OF MUSLIM CULTURES: Collect examples of folk tales (Inea Bushnaq's *Arab Folktales*, Pantheon Books, 1986) and other renditions of folktales from Muslim regions, children's books (preferably in Arabic or other languages known to the students), jokes (*Goha*, Denys Johnson-Davies, transl., Hoopoe Books, 1993), and songs (many of which are on cassette tapes) from various Muslim countries and regions. Public libraries have good collections, as do Muslim book sellers. Parents are also a good source of jokes and stories, and they may be encouraged to record one on cassette for the class. Listen to readings and songs, and discuss ways in which the stories and jokes reflect city and country life. What clues does the literature contain about the landscape, plants, animals and climate of the region? What clues do the stories, songs and jokes give about family life? What lessons and values about Islam can you find in the stories? How are they similar and different?

ACQUIRING SKILLS / ENRICHMENT:

6. MAKING DIFFERENT TYPES OF HEADGEAR: Worksheets #9 and #10 contain patterns for making Central Asian embroidered caps and Omani embroidered caps traditionally worn by men. Some of these hats are also adapted for use by women, in which they are worn atop a silk scarf or veil. The hats may be made of synthetic or wool felt, muslin, or even durable paper. They may be decorated with stitchery, glued- or stitched-on appliqué, beads or sequin designs, paint or crayons. The teacher may also help the students make other types of traditional headgear from various Muslim regions, such as the Arab *kuffiyeh* and *agal* (see catalogue of resources from AWAIR, 1865 Euclid Ave., Suite 4, Berkeley CA 94709), the Tuareg head-wrap, or any of the various *hejab* fashions worn by urban or rural women in the Muslim world.

7. ARTS AND CRAFTS FROM MUSLIM LANDS: Collect information, samples and pictures on traditional arts and crafts from Muslim lands. These may include rugs, bric-a-brac, wall plaques, clothing, hats, leather goods, mats, ceramics, etc. Have the students work in groups to ADAPT OR SIMULATE SOME OF THESE CRAFTS to materials found in home or school. Art teachers in the school may be willing to assist on more complicated projects. Detergent bottles may be decorated as ceramics, heavy brown paper may imitate wood or leather, and cardboard boxes may be covered with paper cut-outs to simulate mosaics. Fabric painting or simple stitchery invokes embroidery, though more complex projects are a good skill-enhancing activity. Plastic or fabric scrim, yarn and crochet hooks can be used to simulate the art of rug-knotting. For references on Islamic geometric designs, Dover Publications, Inc., 31 East 2nd St., Mineola, NY 11501 publishes several excellent color design books. CALLIGRAPHY projects can be done in fancy paper. Write an Arabic word, *du'a* or verse in pencil. Trace the writing in white glue. Pour metallic glitter over the glue and shake off excess. The designs may be mounted on paper lace doilies, borders, or framed. The idea of a project to produce craft items for sale is a very ambitious one that might better be taken up as an extracurricular project under the guidance of an interested parent or other volunteer.

8. PLAN A HERITAGE FAIR, BAZAAR OR PARTY using some of the ideas modeled on the culminating activity sketched out in this unit. The scale can vary from a simple class activity to a community festival. It may involve fund-raising for the school or for charity. The important feature of the event is its capacity to motivate group and individual activity, to stimulate the desire to excel and to spread the cooperative learning experience to benefit other members of the school and community.

UNIT REVIEW AND EVALUATION ACTIVITIES

Review: This section provides a summary of selected review and enrichment activities that have been described in specific sections of the teaching suggestions, above. They may be more convenient to implement at the end of the unit, where they will help to tie together important aspects of the learning experience. Several additional activities are suggested. An overview of activities and project instructions for the Heritage Fair is given.

Evaluation: A creative teacher will find ways to use and adapt many of the lesson activities described here as assessment tools. A student portfolio of maps, projects, learning logs, and worksheets would best document the student's involvement with and mastery of the unit objectives. At the end of this segment, a test question file is provided. The teacher can select several questions from each section to make a traditional assessment tool based upon the specific text sections, concepts and themes covered in classwork.

Answer Keys: Answers to section questions, worksheets and the test question file begin on page 124.

UNIT REVIEW

1. MAPPING FROM MEMORY: Use Worksheets #1a–c to make a map from memory. Color and cut out each of the continent outlines. Using a sheet of blue or white 11" x 17" paper (or other large paper from a roll), fold it in half lengthwise and draw a line in the fold for the equator. Have students arrange the continents on the map from memory. Then, have them check their placement with a world map. Check each student's map for correct placement, then have them glue down the continents and decorate their maps with ships, compass rose, borders, etc.

2. MAP CONCENTRATION GAME: To reinforce the information given in this lesson, a kind of "Concentration" can later be played in small groups. Practice locating physical features like rivers, mountain ranges, deserts and bodies of water. Then study the map carefully. Using the eastern hemisphere of a large physical map as a base, cover each continent with numbered 3"–4" (10 cm) squares of cardboard. Use the list of "Places to Remember" at the end of the student text, and have the students add to it. Then, one student or the teacher calls out the name of a geographic feature, and the student must lift the correct cardboard square. First try gets 10 points, second try 5 points, third 1 point. After three tries, another student gets to try. The one with the highest score after 10 rounds wins.

3. RIVER RIDDLES: Use Worksheet #4 to identify major rivers in Muslim regions. It would be very beneficial to have the students locate the rivers (and some additional ones) on an unlabelled outline map, such as those found in teaching aids and supplemental workbooks.

4. **LEARNING LANDFORMS:** Use a standard landforms chart to study, then quiz students on the names and definitions of various landforms. The class might draw a landforms chart or make a model from clay or flour/salt dough and tempera paints.

5. **LOCATING MUSLIM COUNTRIES ON A MAP:** The teacher may use the blank outline map with countries (Worksheet #12) in several ways.

   a. Ask students to shade in, or otherwise mark, as many majority Muslim countries as they can recall in Africa, Europe and Asia. This is a good evaluation activity. Score the number of correctly identified out of approximately 50 (the sources do not agree on population figures), allowing 1/2 point for including countries with large minorities, if included.

   b. Instead of shading, or in addition to it, have students label as many majority Muslim countries as they can from memory. They may also develop a key for designating countries with large minorities.

6. **LOCATING AND IDENTIFYING MAJOR CITIES:** After studying the cities on *The Muslim World Map* or atlases, use Worksheet #6 to fill in the blanks. This could be a game or a quiz. The teacher may adjust the level of difficulty by covering some of the cities when photocopying the worksheet.

7. **DEVELOPMENT WORD WEB:** See Teaching Suggestions for Section 6, Activity #4 for suggested categories. It is not expected that students will attain a deep understanding of the concept at this level, but they can obtain an introductory notion. Build upon the students' fund of conceptual knowledge about important activities within a country or a community, starting from simple questions about transportation, communication, acquiring and using natural resources, education, health, products and services. Discuss what roles governments and individuals can play in building a country. Discuss why development is important, and how it is related to citizens' way of life (or, in adult parlance, *standard of living*).

8. **RESOURCES, JOBS AND PRODUCTS:** Use Worksheet #11 to make a graphic organizer, summarizing information about various types of resources and how they affect the economy of a country or region. The activity may be expanded by asking students to choose one resource listed to discuss how its use affects the environment. Students may also choose a resource that is traded internationally, discussing how it affects life in other countries, and/or how its use worldwide affects the environment.

9. **ENERGY ALTERNATIVES (science crossover):** An interesting and important theme that might provide correlations with science lessons is the natural resource **sunshine**, related to the location of most of the majority Muslim countries. The teacher may profitably weave in lessons from earth science about the year-round availability of sunshine and the resulting potential both for solar energy use and for agriculture (if sufficient supplies of water can be found). This theme is important for the entire region. Some students may wish to do science projects on solar energy, agriculture in dry regions (including new methods of irrigation, new *halophyte* crops grown in sea water, and underground water supplies, or *aquifers*).

OVERVIEW—HERITAGE FAIR PROJECTS OR STUDENT PORTFOLIOS

Throughout the student text of this unit, various student projects are described. By Section 8, the model class described in the script has made classroom exhibits and decided to display them for the whole school. Eventually, the class decides to invite guests. The projects mentioned in the text are listed here, with some additional ideas and instructions.

Some of these projects are most suitable for individual or small-group work, while a few can be done by the whole class. Each student may assemble a portfolio of work to be assessed for a final grade on this unit. The teacher will prepare a list of items needed to complete the portfolio. Among these items, students may be asked to do one or more projects of their own choosing, following certain criteria. **Worksheet #9 has been developed to assist students and teachers in organizing these projects step by step.** For example, they may be asked to do three projects, one each related to art, literature and geography, each involving use of readily-available library research materials. The following list provides suggestions and references to the text or teachers' section or worksheet # where instructions are given:

- Make a drawing or model of a house, masjid or other building (Sections 4 and 7).

- Make an info-cube on a famous city in a Muslim country (or a famous person?) (Section 5).

- Collect cooking recipes from Muslim regions and map the origin of the ingredients (Sections 4 and 8, see question #1).

- Make Central Asian hats or other headgear from a specific Muslim culture (Section 8, Worksheet #10).

- Make a drawing or dress a doll in the traditional dress of a Muslim country or region (Section 8; see question #2).

- Make a Resource Map mural with pictographs to represent important products, industries or attractions in a region. This is an expansion of the underground resource map described in Section 4 and Worksheet #7. Individuals or small groups may work on smaller regions, but the result may be a large mural map of Muslim regions in Asia, Africa and Europe. The class will develop a standard key of symbols. Use the outline map of countries, which can be enlarged, or purchase a large poster map.

- Make a poster describing an environmental issue in a Muslim region (Section 4).

- Make a poster describing an area of conflict (Section 7; see illustration in text).

- Make a poster describing an interesting occupation in Muslim countries (Section 6).

- Make a travel brochure or display. Develop an itinerary for a tour of Muslim countries, featuring tourist attractions and points of interest (Section 5).

- Select a short story, joke, poem or other literature to recite or act out or illustrate (Section 8).

- Make a poster about Muslim unity or tolerance in Islam, collecting relevant verses from the Qur'an and Hadith, as well as stories from Islamic history (see stories and other material from IQRA International Education Foundation and the Islamic Foundation) that illustrate examples of these two qualities.

- Make a calligraphy or geometric design in any artisitic medium, or make a poster describing the designs in a specific building (Sections 7 and 8).

- Learn about and demonstrate a famous craft from Muslim countries (Section 8; see question #4).

- Design a charity project, collecting food, clothing, money or other items for a local community. If your school is planning a Heritage Fair, Community Bazaar, etc., such, as the one modeled in Section 7 of this unit, a table for such fund-raising (bake sale, toy sale, display for charity, etc.) could be a part of the activity. Another interesting project that involves no direct transmission of money is to establish contact with Muslim children in one of these areas, sending them letters, drawings or other artwork; copies of the Qur'an; audio- or videocassette tapes containing stories, songs or personal introductions (Section 7).

TEST QUESTION FILE: Photocopiable questions for selection are placed at the end of the worksheet section, Part IV. Answer key follows this Unit Review section, from page 122.

ANSWER KEYS

SECTION 1

1. Why do people who share a common way of life often live close together? *They like to share community activities and family life with people similar to themselves.*

2. What is the total world population? *Approximately five billion people (actual figure in Dorling Kindersley Reference Atlas is 5.4 billion).* Write in numbers. *5,000,000,000.* Write the Muslim population of the world in numbers. *About 1,000,000,000.* How many zeros does the number have? *Nine zeros.*

SECTION 2

1. What does the map key show? *It shows what the map's symbols or colors mean.*

2. What does *percent* mean? *It means "how many out of one hundred (100)."*

3. In what library resources can you find out the population of each country in the world? *In an atlas or encyclopedia.* Pick three countries. Write the name of each and its population. *Answers vary.*

4. How can you use the *Map of the Muslim World* to estimate, or guess, how many Muslims are in each country, if you know the total population? *Look at the highest and lowest percent for the color of the country. Multiply the population by both percent figures. That way, you can get the highest and lowest numbers of Muslims.*

5. CALCULATOR ACTIVITY: What is the highest and the lowest possible number of Muslims in Nigeria? *Based on a 1994 atlas, population of Nigeria is 90 million. The map shows over 50%. The lowest population is 45 million, the highest is 90 million (or 100%, which is not true, as there are many Christians in Nigeria, and traditional religions).* Try some other countries. *See above.*

SECTION 3

1. Physical maps show *landforms, bodies of water* and *kinds of natural vegetation (plants or climate areas).*

2. Name two important rivers in Africa and two in Asia. Make a chart listing all of the countries that each flows through. *Answers vary, see text and maps.*

3. Name three African countries with many mountains. *Ethiopia, Kenya, Morocco, Algeria, etc.*

4. Name the bodies of water that surround the Arabian Peninsula. *Mediterranean Sea, Red Sea, Persian/Arabian Gulf, Arabian Sea.*

5. List five Muslim countries that are nearly all desert. *Egypt, Libya, Algeria, Mauritania, Saudi Arabia, Turkmenistan, Uzbekistan, etc.*

6. List three Muslim countries that are very mountainous. *Iran, Turkey, Afghanistan, Morocco, Tajikstan, Kyrgyzstan, Azerbaijan, etc.*

7. Compare the land and climate in North Africa and Southeast Asia. *North Africa is mostly desert, but Southeast Asia is mostly tropical rain forest. Both areas have some mountains and hills; both are near the sea. Southeast Asia is near the equator, but North Africa is outside the tropics.*

Thinking a little harder:

a. Write a paragraph about the land and climate in Muslim lands. In a few sentences, describe what you learned from the students' reports. *Answers vary.*

SECTION 4

1. Why is water the most important resource in many Muslim regions? *Water is scarce in many Muslim regions, and people cannot live without it.*

2. Name some important uses for water, and ways to get it. *Drinking, washing and growing food. Water can come as rain, in rivers or from underground, or people can take the salt out of sea water.*

3. List some products you use that come from each continent. *Answers vary, based on products listed in text.*

4. Make a chart of some minerals named on the map in the section. Draw pictures of things that are made with these minerals. *Answers vary.*

5. List some **fresh** foods and **processed** foods that you ate yesterday. *Answers vary.*

6. Mark the following products that are consumer goods:

__ cement mixer	✔ pair of jeans	__ dump truck	✔ shirt
✔ washing machine	✔ computer	✔ television	✔ toy
__ cement	__ hospital bed	✔ bicycle	__ tractor ✔ pencil

SECTION 5

1. What is a port city? *A city where ships stop to load or unload.* Why do some cities become important ports? *Port cities often have good harbors, good location on transportation routes, or both.*

2. Name some places in the world that attract tourists. *Answers vary.*

3. Write about the place where you live. What is important about its location? (Ask your parents or teacher to help you find out.) *Answers vary; teachers may wish to make this a mini-research project to explore local geography.*

SECTION 6

1. Name four kinds of service workers that help you. *Teachers, bus drivers, restaurant workers, doctors, etc.*

2. What can governments do so that they to have more skilled workers in a country? *They can help improve training and education, or they can help attract workers from overseas, etc.*

3. Think about, or talk to someone whose job is in a different country. Write a list of advantages and disadvantages of working far from home. *Answers vary.*

SECTION 7

1. Draw a picture or write about a masjid you might build. What would it look like? Where would you like to build it? What resources will you use in the building? *Answers vary.*

2. Write a diary of a Muslim for one day. Mention all of the things that Muslims everywhere do in the same way each day. *Prayer, wudu', du'a, avoiding haram foods and behavior, etc.* What things do all Muslims do each year in the same way? *Fast during Ramadan, celebrate two 'Ids, make hajj, attend prayers at masjid, etc.*

3. What languages are spoken in your home? Are they different from the ones you speak at school? What alphabets do you use to write? *Answers vary.*

4. Why are teachers important in a Muslim community? What subjects do they teach? *Teachers help adults and children to learn about Islam and many other subjects. They might teach Arabic, Qur'an, and other Islamic subjects. They might teach any subject like science, math, art or anything else that is needed.*

5. Make a list of important things that each Muslim community needs to do. Beside each item, suggest how children can help to do them. *Answers vary.*

6. Learn more about a country where Muslims are suffering hardship. Collect newspaper and magazine clippings. Ask your parents to help find television programs about it. Ask your teacher or librarian to help you find books and other sources. Make a report to the class. *Answers vary.*

SECTION 8

1. Pick your family's favorite recipe, or a favorite processed food. Make a list of the ingredients in it. Find out where these products are grown. *Answers vary.*

2. Find out about the traditional dress of a country not mentioned here. Draw a picture or dress a figure for display. *Answers vary.*

3. Find a joke, a poem or a story to tell to the group. Name the country where it was first recited, and tell whether it is very old or more modern. *Answers vary.*

4. List some famous crafts from Muslim countries. Bring some examples from home with your parents' permission. Do a report or project on how these crafts are made. (Examples: leather work, knotting rugs, dyeing cloth, pottery, knitting, embroidery, calligraphy, metalwork, jewelry.) *Answers vary.*

TEST QUESTION FILE KEY

MATCHING SECTION:

A. Identifying Countries
Find at least two countries in the list that fit the description. Write the matching letters in the space.

1. b, c, f, m, q [countries that have petroleum]
2. c, f, i, j, m, n, o, q [desert countries]
3. All but China (e) and India (g) [Muslim majority countries]
4. e, g [important Muslim minority countries]
5. a, e, f, g, h, l, m, o, p, q [countries in Asia]
6. c, j, k, n [countries in Africa]
7. b, d [countries in Europe]

B. Words to Remember
Match the words from column 1 to the correct definition in column 2.

1. e
2. c
3. g
4. k
5. h
6. f
7. j
8. d
9. b
10. i
11. l
12. a

FILL IN THE BLANKS SECTION:

1. tropical wet
2. plateau
3. physical map
4. a green place in the desert with water
5. mountain range
6. source; mouth
7. census
8. key
9. majority
10. minority
11. culture

MULTIPLE CHOICE SECTION:

1. b—importing goods
2. c—exporting goods
3. c—majority
4. a—minority
5. a—consumer
6. a—history

MAP SKILLS SECTION: *SEE LABELLED MAPS IN STUDENT TEXT*

1. Continent map/Eastern Hemisphere outline map: Shade in the approximate areas of Africa and Asia where Muslims are the majority.

2. Country outline maps of Africa and Asia: Label as many countries as you know, or color and label countries with Muslim majorities.

3. World outline map: Label continents, oceans and other bodies of water.

4. Bonus: Country outline map of Europe—Find two Muslim countries in Europe and label .them.

THEME QUESTIONS SECTION:

1. Location: *Answers vary.*
2. Resources: *Answers vary*
3. Living as minority or majority: *Answers vary.*
4. The Muslim world community *(ummah)*: *Answers vary.*
5. Development: *Answers vary.*

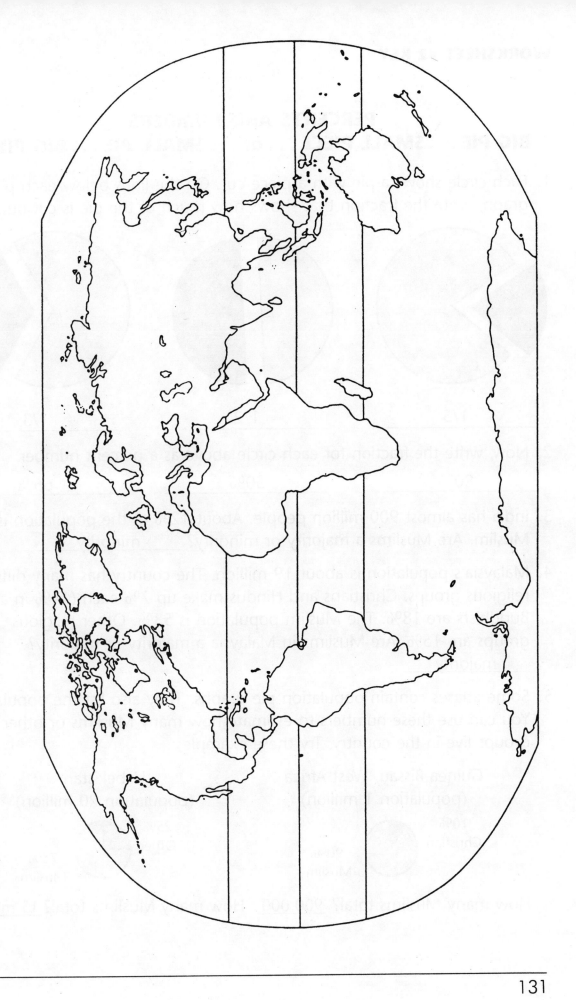

PERCENTS AND NUMBERS
BIG PIE... SMALL PIECE... or... SMALL PIE... BIG PIECE

1. Each circle shows a pie with a piece cut. On the lines below each pie graph, write the fraction that shows how much of the pie is cut out.

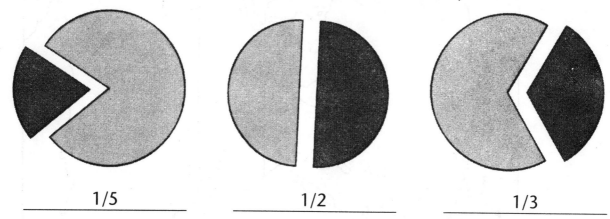

1/5	1/2	1/3

2. Now, write the fraction for each circle above as a percent number.

80%	50%	66%

3. India has almost 900 million people. About 12% of the population is Muslim. Are Muslims a majority or minority? _____minority_____

4. Malaysia's population is about 19 million. The country has many different religious groups. Christians and Hindus make up 7% each (14% in all). Buddhists are 18%. The Muslim population is 53%. Other religious groups are 15%. Are Muslims in Malaysia a majority or minority?
_____majority_____

5. Some atlases contain population pie graphs. They also list the population. You can use these numbers to estimate how many Muslims or other groups live in the country. Try these examples:

Guinea-Bissau, West Africa
(population 1 million)

10% Christian   90% Muslim

Uzbekistan
(population 20 million)

25% Other   75% Muslim

How many Muslims total? 900,000   How many Muslims total? 15 million

RIVER RIDDLES

Guess the name of these important rivers in Muslim regions from the clues. In blank A, write the name of the river. In blank B, write the name of the continent where the river is located.

1. The longest river in the world, its name rhymes with "smile."

   A _____Nile River_____   B _____Africa_____

2. Two rivers flow into the drying Aral Sea; their names sound like "How are ya!"

   A_1 _____Syr Dar'ya River_____   B _____Asia_____

   A_2 _____Amu Dar'ya River_____

3. A river that flows in a rainbow shape brings water to the desert edge. Its name looks like the cat with stripes.

   A _____Niger River_____   B _____Africa_____

4. An ocean, a country and a river all have names whose first three letters are the same.

   A _____Indus River_____   B _____Asia_____

5. Twin rivers' source lies in Turkey. They meet before flowing into a gulf that has two names (Persian and Arabian).

   A_1 _____Tigris River_____   B _____Asia_____

   A_2 _____Euphrates River_____

6. A holy river for the Hindu religion, its mouth is in a small Muslim country that begins with a "B."

   A _____Ganges River_____   B _____Asia_____

Part IV

Worksheets, Projects and Evaluation Activities

Words to Remember

calligraphy = decorative writing

census = a survey to gather information about people in a country

climate = the weather in a place over a long time

dam = a wall built across a river to store water

energy = power to do work

geography = our study of the world, its land and people

irrigation = bringing water to crops

key = box or sign on a map that tells what the map means

natural gas = fuel resource from underground

mountain range = a chain or group of mountains

mouth = place where a river empties into a larger body of water

oasis = a green place in the desert with water

percent = how many out of every hundred (100)

petroleum = crude oil as it comes from the ground

physical map = map that shows the shape of the land and what grows on it

plateau = high, flat land

population = the number of people

port city = a city where ships stop to load and unload

processing = changing a resource or product in some way

qanat = underground canals for water

resource = something that people use

source = the beginning of a river

textiles = fabrics

tourist = visitor who comes to see a place

tropical wet = a warm, wet climate

Ideas to Remember

consumers = people who use products or resources or services

culture = way of life

development = building a country to help its people

export goods = products sold to another country

history = the story of a place or people over time

independent = countries that have their own government

industry = a group of factories making products

import goods = products bought from another country

location = place, where a thing is

majority = more than one-half of something

minority = less than one-half of something

region = a part of the world

service job = doing work that people pay for (contrast with: production job)

ummah = the Muslim community in a place or in the world

Places to Remember

East Africa

North Africa

Central Asia

South Asia

Southeast Asia

Southwest Asia

Learn the names of some Muslim countries in each region listed above

CONTINENT CUT-OUTS

Label each continent. Choose a different color crayon or marker to fill in each continent. Cut out the shapes carefully. Arrange them on a large sheet of blue construction paper (18" x 24" or 45cm x 60cm) with a horizontal line in the middle for the EQUATOR. After your teacher has checked the position of your continents, glue them carefully to the paper. Label the oceans between your continents. Add a compass rose in the corner. Add any decorations you like to your map, such as a border, sailing ships, etc.

CONTINENT CUT-OUTS (continued)

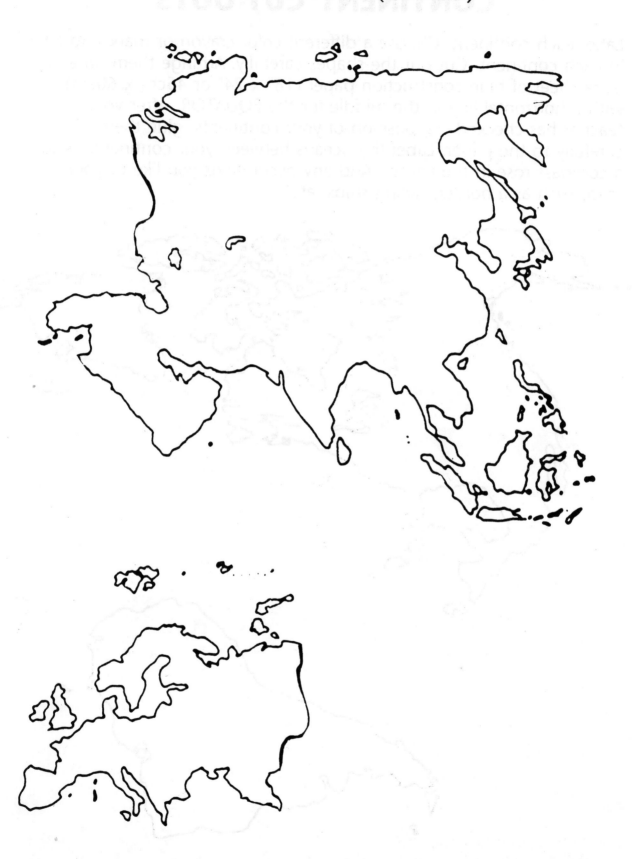

CONTINENT CUT-OUTS (continued)

PERCENTS AND NUMBERS
BIG PIE...SMALL PIECE...or...SMALL PIE...BIG PIECE

1. Each circle shows a pie with a piece cut. On the lines below each pie graph, write the fraction that shows how much of the pie is cut out.

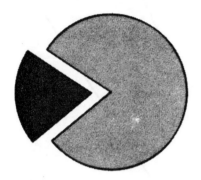   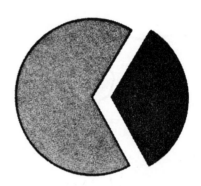

_____   _____   _____

2. Now, write the fraction for each circle above as a percent number.

_____   _____   _____

3. India has almost 900 million people. About 12% of the population is Muslim. Are Muslims a majority or minority? _____

4. Malaysia's population is about 19 million. The country has many different religious groups. Christians and Hindus make up 7% each (14% in all). Buddhists are 18%. The Muslim population is 53%. Other religious groups are 15%. Are Muslims in Malaysia a majority or minority?_____

5. Some atlases contain population pie graphs. They also list the population. You can use these numbers to estimate how many Muslims or other groups live in the country. Try these examples:

Guinea-Bissau, West Africa
(population 1 million)

How many Muslims total?_____

Uzbekistan
(population 20 million)

How many Muslims total?_____

WHAT IS THE *UMMAH*?

A. Trace the Arabic script of the word *ummah*. Use the space to write the word in Arabic yourself.

_____ أُمَّه _____

B. Write a poem describing the *ummah,* and its definition "community," starting the first word of each line with a letter of the word.

U _____

M _____

M _____

A _____

H _____

C _____

O _____

M _____

M _____

U _____

N _____

I _____

T _____

Y _____

RIVER RIDDLES

Guess the name of these important rivers in Muslim regions from the clues. In blank A, write the name of the river. In blank B, write the name of the continent where the river is located.

1. The longest river in the world, its name rhymes with "smile."

   A _____   B _____

2. Two rivers flow into the drying Aral Sea; their names sound like "How are ya!"

   A_1 _____   B _____

   A_2 _____

3. A river that flows in a rainbow shape brings water to the desert edge. Its name looks like the cat with stripes.

   A _____   B _____

4. An ocean, a country and a river all have names whose first three letters are the same.

   A _____   B _____

5. Twin rivers' source lies in Turkey. They meet before flowing into a gulf that has two names (Persian and Arabian).

   A_1 _____   B _____

   A_2 _____

6. A holy river for the Hindu religion, its mouth is in a small Muslim country that begins with a "B."

   A _____   B _____

MAKE AN INFO-CUBE ON IMPORTANT CITIES IN MUSLIM REGIONS

Select a city in a Muslim country. Look up information about it in encyclopedias, atlases or other books. Use the information to make an info-cube. Copy the diagram below, enlarging it 200%, or draw it at least twice as large as shown, or more. Paste or copy it onto heavy paper. On each of the six sides that will show on the folded cube, write or draw pictures giving the information from #1–6, below, showing the following information on each of the six sides. Fold the cube as shown. Hang a string from one corner to display.

These are the topics for each side of the info-cube:

1. Name of city, country, important river or other location

   _____

   _____

   _____

2. Population, area, whether it is a capital

   _____

3. Important jobs in the city

   _____

   _____

4. A short, famous story about the city

   _____

   _____

   _____

   _____

5. One or more famous buildings or places

   _____

6. Facts about a famous Muslim from the city

   _____

   _____

LAYOUT AND DIRECTIONS FOR MAKING AN INFO-CUBE

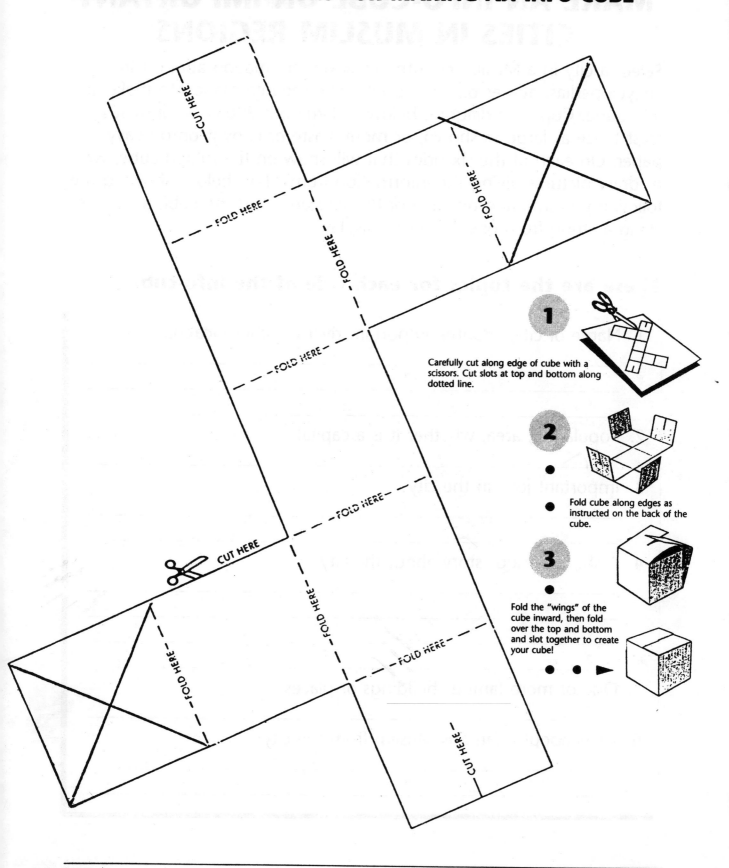

1 Carefully cut along edge of cube with a scissors. Cut slots at top and bottom along dotted line.

2 Fold cube along edges as instructed on the back of the cube.

3 Fold the "wings" of the cube inward, then fold over the top and bottom and slot together to create your cube!

NAME THESE CITIES

Use your memory or the "Map of the Muslim World" to fill in the city names on the outline map.

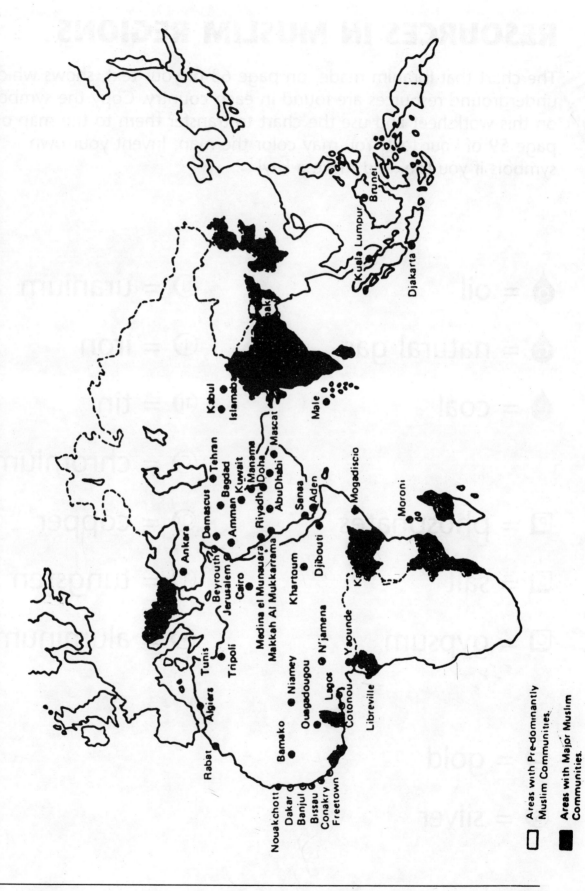

Areas with Pre-dominantly
Muslim Communities.

Areas with Major Muslim
Communities.

RESOURCES IN MUSLIM REGIONS

The chart that Ibrahim made, on page 63 of your text, shows which underground resources are found in each country. Copy the symbols on this worksheet and use the chart to transfer them to the map on page 59 of your text. You may color the map. Invent your own symbols if you like, and make a key!

🌢 = oil

🌢 = natural gas

🌢 = coal

Ⓟ = phosphates

Ⓢ = salt

Ⓖ = gypsum

Ⓖ = gold

Ⓢ = silver

Ⓤ = uranium

Ⓘ = iron

Ⓣⓘ = tin

Ⓒ = chromium

Ⓒⓤ = copper

Ⓣ = tungsten

Ⓐ = aluminum

CITIES AND LANDFORMS

Use an atlas or wall chart with physical maps or relief maps to locate the landforms and bodies of water near 10 cities in Muslim regions. Then fill in the chart with the information you have gathered. Compare with your classmates' results.

Continent	Name of City	Nearby Geographic Features

PLANNING HERITAGE FAIR OR PORTFOLIO PROJECTS

Choose one or more projects from the categories your teacher describes:

1. Making a drawing, art project or model for display:

What object will I build, make or draw? _____

In which country is this object located? _____

What books and magazines will I use to learn about the object?

_____

_____

_____

2. Making a poster:

What is the subject of my poster? _____

_____

What books, magazines and newspapers will I use to learn about the subject?

_____

_____

_____

3. Telling a joke, poem or story from Muslim lands:

What is the title? _____

I found the work in this book: _____

_____

In which country or region did the work originate? _____

Write a short summary of the joke, poem or story here: _____

_____

_____

_____

_____

_____

_____

_____

_____

_____

PATTERN FOR MAKING CENTRAL ASIAN HATS

1. Carefully cut out the pattern.
2. Lay it on a piece of heavy construction paper, brown paper, felt or other cloth.
3. Trace around the edges with chalk.
4. Cut cloth or paper on chalk lines, taking care to stay on the lines.
5. Repeat four times to make four sections of the hat.
6. Decorate each section with paint, appliqué or embroidery designs.
7. Sew, staple or glue along dotted lines, adjusting the hat to fit you.

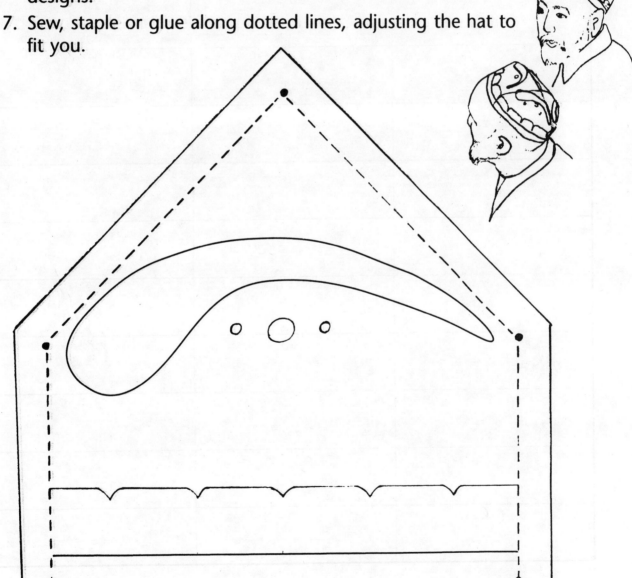

WHAT DO RESOURCES MAKE?

Use the chart below to organize ideas about using resources. List a resource from Muslim lands in each box of column 1, using the text, Sections 4 and 5. In column 2, list the jobs that come from working with this resource. In column 3, list the products that are made from the resource. The example will get you started.

1. RESOURCE	2. JOBS	3. PRODUCTS
grazing animals (sheep, cattle, goats, etc.)	shepherds, dairy workers, butchers, leather & textile workers	wool, cloth, rugs, leather products, meat, dairy products

BLANK OUTLINE MAP WITH COUNTRIES

TEST QUESTION FILE

MATCHING SECTION:

A. Identifying Countries

Find at least two countries in the list that fit the description. Write the matching letters in the space.

1. Countries that have petroleum _____

2. Desert countries _____

3. Muslim majority countries _____

4. Important Muslim minority countries_____

5. Countries in Asia_____

6. Countries in Africa _____

7. Countries in Europe _____

    a) Afghanistan
    b) Albania
    c) Algeria
    d) Bosnia-Herzegovina
    e) China
    f) Iran
    g) India
    h) Kazakhstan
    i) Kuwait
    j) Mali
    k) Morocco
    l) Palestine
    m) Saudi Arabia
    n) Sudan
    o) Syria
    p) Turkey
    q) Uzbekistan

B. Words to Remember

Match the words from column 1 to the correct definition in column 2.

1. _____ calligraphy   a) anything that people use
2. _____ climate   b) the number of people
3. _____ dam   c) the weather in a place over a long time
4. _____ energy   d) crude oil as it comes from the ground
5. _____ irrigation   e) decorative writing
6. _____ natural gas   f) fuel resource that burns cleanly
7. _____ percent   g) a wall built across a river to store water
8. _____ petroleum   h) bringing water to crops
9. _____ population   i) a city where ships stop to load and unload
10. _____ port city   j) how many out of every hundred (100)
11. _____ processing   k) power to do work
12. _____ resource   l) changing a resource or product in some way

FILL IN THE BLANKS SECTION:

1. A warm climate with lots of rainfall is _____.

2. High, flat land is called a _____.

3. A _____ shows the shape of the land and what grows on it.

4. An oasis is _____.

5. A chain or a group of mountains is called a _____.

6. A river begins at its _____, and it empties into a larger body of water at its _____.

7. Governments take a _____ to gather information about people living in the country.

8. The _____ is the part of a map that tells what the symbols or colors on the map mean.

9. A _____ means more than one-half of the people belonging to a group.

10. A _____ means less than one-half of the people belonging to a group.

11. People's traditions, like dress, food, houses and daily habits are part of their way of life, called _____.

MULTIPLE CHOICE SECTION:

1. When people buy products from another country, they are _____.
   a. processing goods   b. importing goods   c. exporting goods

2. When people sell products to another country, they are _____.
   a. processing goods   b. importing goods   c. exporting goods

3. A country named the Sudan has 70% Muslims and 30% Christians and other religious groups. In the Sudan, Muslims are a _____.
   a. minority   b. tourists   c. majority

4. A country named India has 80% Hindus, 10% Muslims and 10% other religious groups. In India, Muslims are the _____.
   a. minority   b. tourists   c. majority

5. When you buy things at the store and use resources at home, you are a _____.
   a. consumer   b. service worker   c. producer   d. tourist

6. The story of a place or people over time is its_____.
   a. history   b. culture   c. resource

MAP SKILLS SECTION:

1. Continent map/Eastern Hemisphere outline map:
   Shade in the approximate areas of Africa and Asia where Muslims are the majority.

2. Country outline maps of Africa and Asia:
   Label as many countries as you know, or color and label countries with Muslim majorities.
   Bonus: Country outline map of Europe—Find two Muslim countries in Europe and label them.
3. World outline map:
   Label continents, oceans and other bodies of water.

THEME QUESTIONS SECTION:

1. *Location:* On the world map, choose a location where you would like to build a city. Tell what makes it a good location. Describe what jobs and activities will take place there.

2. *Resources:* Choose a country you have studied. Describe two resources found there, and tell how they are used, and how they help the country.

3. *Living as minority or majority:* How should Muslims behave toward others when they live among people of other religions and cultures? Describe how your life is different if you are a member of a majority or a minority.

4. *The Muslim world community (**ummah**):* Compare what you knew about the *ummah* before studying this unit and now. How have your ideas changed about where Muslims live in the world today?

5. *Development:* List four ways in which people work to develop their communities and countries. Tell how each kind of effort helps people to have a better life.

NOTES